Science, Bread, and Circuses

Science, Bread, and Circuses

Folkloristic Essays on Science for the Masses

Gregory Schrempp

UTAH STATE UNIVERSITY PRESS
Logan

© 2014 by the University Press of Colorado

Published by Utah State University Press
An imprint of University Press of Colorado
5589 Arapahoe Avenue, Suite 206C
Boulder, Colorado 80303

 The University Press of Colorado is a proud member of
The Association of American University Presses.

The University Press of Colorado is a cooperative publishing enterprise supported, in part,
by Adams State University, Colorado State University, Fort Lewis College, Metropolitan
State University of Denver, Regis University, University of Colorado, University of Northern
Colorado, Utah State University, and Western State Colorado University.

ISBN: 978-0-87421-969-2 (paper)
ISBN: 978-0-87421-970-8 (ebook)

Library of Congress Cataloging-in-Publication Data

Schrempp, Gregory Allen, 1950–
    Science, bread, and circuses : folkloristic essays on science for the masses / Gregory Schrempp.
        pages cm
    ISBN 978-0-87421-969-2 (paperback) — ISBN 978-0-87421-970-8 (ebook)
    1. Science in popular culture. 2. Folklore. 3. Legends. 4. Myths. I. Title.
    Q172.5.P65S45 2014
    303.48'3—dc23
                                    2014001149

The material in chapter 1 was published in earlier form as "Formulas of Conversion: Proverbial
    Approaches to Technological and Scientific Exposition" (Midwestern Folklore 31:5–13) and
    is used by permission of the Hoosier Folklore Society.
The material in chapter 2 was published in earlier form as "Canonizing Creativity: Folkloric
    Patterns in Motivational Speaking" (Midwestern Folklore 33:37–43) and is used by permis-
    sion of the Hoosier Folklore Society.
The material in chapter 4 was published in earlier form as "Taking the Dawkins Challenge, or,
    The Dark Side of the Meme" (Journal of Folklore Research 46:91–100) and is used by per-
    mission of Indiana University Press.

Cover illustration: © gualtiero boffi / Shutterstock

Contents

Acknowledgments

I am grateful to the many students and colleagues who provided thoughtful and helpful responses to the ideas presented in this book. I am especially thankful to Ronald Baker, Karen Duffy, William Hansen, Wally Hooper, Jens Lund, Moira Marsh, Nan McEntire, Joseph Nagy, Elliott Oring, Daniel Peretti, Marshall Sahlins, Bill Schrempp, George Stocking, and Kyoim Yun. The UCLA Film and Television Archive provided assistance with the film research. I am grateful to Michael Spooner and the staff of Utah State University Press/University Press of Colorado for their support and help; reports from two anonymous readers were also very useful. My wife, Cornelia Fales, helped with every aspect of this endeavor.

Science, Bread, and Circuses

Introduction

*B*READ AND CIRCUSES IS A PEJORATIVE PHRASE, BUT who would give up either? The term *folklore* is often used derogatorily; but in a recent, elite university class I got *no* "yeses" to this question: would a world without urban legends be a better world? And who among us is not proud, sometimes, to merge into "the masses," or at least this or that "mass"?

The works that most epitomize the contemporary genre of popular science—books by John Barrow, Daniel Dennett, Brian Greene, or Stephen Hawking—are not read by "the masses" but instead by the proverbial "serious reader" who maintains a generalized philosophical or nerdy interest in science. The very notion of the popular is relative, begging the question, how popular? The book you are now reading, though designed to be complete in itself, is also a companion to a previous work, *The Ancient Mythology of Modern Science: A Mythologist Looks (Seriously) at Popular Science Writing* (Schrempp 2012a). In that work I critically analyze the arguments put forward in major books by writers like those just mentioned, who form what might be termed (oxymoronically for sure) the elite of the popular science genre. What remains for consideration is a vast, variegated, fascinating landscape of science popularizing. It would be a great mistake to limit one's gaze to the elite realm, which forms only one small part of the venture.

The strategies of science popularizing—or science domestication—that I focus on in the chapters in this book have all been selected with a folklorist's eye for traditional gestures and genres that have always radiated power and appeal; these include major oral narrative genres (myth, epic, legend, folktale) as well as other orally inspired forms (such as proverb, sermon, and local religious visions and rituals/spectacles).[1] For some time, however, folklorists have recognized that research on such genres today frequently leads, imperceptibly, into popular cultural transformations of them, whether in film, literature, or food fashions. I should be clear, therefore, that the folkloristic slant I bring to the topic of popular science is less interested in claiming the emergence of "new forms of folklore" than in calling attention to the persistence of folkloric form, idiom, and worldview within the increasingly important dimension of popular consciousness defined by the impact of

DOI: 10.7330/9780874219708.c000

1

science. My project is thus similar in spirit to what Sandra Dolby (2005) has accomplished in her study of folkloric patterns in contemporary self-help literature, although my study will consider a wider range of artifacts, for books are only one among many media of science popularizing I will consider. Dolby's analysis might be seen, in turn, as a new development within a longer scholarly tradition, advocated by Richard Dorson, among others, of identifying continuities of folklore in realms lying outside traditional oral circulation. My specific concern within this longer tradition will be to identify folkloric inspiration, form, and process in the popular exposition and promotion of science.

"The masses" is a notoriously difficult concept, one I use loosely, evocatively, and provocatively. Three major qualifications should be kept in mind throughout. The first is that the notion of "the masses" is fraught with moral, aesthetic, and political ambivalence, as well as intrinsic reversibility (as are its opposites, "the elite," "the sophisticated"). The masses are low in status but also the basis of all power and often rhapsodized with populist sentiment. The second point is illustrated by a quirk in the term itself, namely, that "the masses" is (are?) plural, in a sense contradicting the direction in which the term seems to be headed—that is, a merging of members into a unitary heap. It will quickly become apparent that we are dealing with more than one mass (and it is probably fair to say that all human beings, if not all living things, belong to a plurality of "lumping" categories). In most cases we are dealing with a polarity straddling a vast borderland. What I mean by "the masses" in this book can most safely be expressed privatively: the works of science popularizing considered here are directed toward audiences whose members lie mostly outside the first circle of devotees of elite popular science literature.

The third point is a combination of the first two: specifically, that some masses are in another respect also elites. Certain artists and critics, most famously Leo Tolstoy, conclude that the greatest art will necessarily be understandable by anyone; in other words, the highest art will necessarily be "low." On this last point, consider the topic of chapter 9, British playwright Tom Stoppard's *Jumpers*. Stoppard is among the very finest writers of dramatic dialogue, backed by a distinguished national/cultural theater tradition; yet much of the dialogue of this play, and certainly the genre-frame, resemble the detective novel, a socially unpretentious literary form radiating the broadest popular appeal. Some of the protagonists are university philosophers, but the action takes place around their activities as amateur acrobats ("jumpers"); and the play opens at a party in which a scantily clad woman swings trapeze-like back and forth above a partying crowd—a sort of circus without a tent. Stoppard's plot also directs attention toward a mission to explore the moon. The mission is made possible by sophisticated technology that, however, also makes possible the real-time viewing of the chosen few space explorers by mass audiences. Moreover, Stoppard's depiction of the technological conquest is punctuated by old, popular romantic songs about the newly demythologized moon. *Jumpers* ruminates on moral quandaries posed by advanced scientific achievement pursued through Falstaffian belly-laughs. If someone wants to claim that *Jumpers* re-contextualizes elite scientific issues not for the masses but for a different elite—a literary elite— I will not argue, though I will point out that Stoppard's elitism inheres at least in part in an impeccable ear for the power of the vulgate.

***

For some, even popular science writing of the elite variety raises concerns about the dilution of science; in the realm we are about to enter, believe me, it gets worse. At the same time, however, there are other intellectual and moral pitfalls to which mass popular science is often less susceptible than the elite forms. Most important, in mass popular science there is typically more transparency about intentions, especially regarding the line at which the science ends and the edification and entertainment begin, and about what non-scientists "really want" from science. In mass popular science we tend to have obvious mythologizing rather than subtle mythologizing; which of these holds greater potential for misleading readers?

On the matter of aesthetic merit, too, I would choose mass popular science (or at least those instances considered here) over elite popular science—although perhaps this is only what one should expect, considering the kinds of talent that are drawn to the two. Putting aside the science, the products considered in the present book are creative and really *fun*. They have "slipped the surly bonds" of gravitas that hold the universe of elite popular science together. Imagine a continuum of strategies for combining science and art: on one end lies an undisguised attempt to use a popular art form as a familiar *vehicle* to carry a new message, while at the other end lies a heady, premature claim to offer a *synthesis* that heals the great divide between science and art, possibly with intimations of offering something higher than science alone. We encounter more of the former strategy in mass popular science and more of the latter in elite popular science. In my judgment, the former more accurately portrays where we really are (still) on the relation of science and art, or, as C. P. Snow famously phrased it, between the "two cultures."

***

As noted, the object of analysis in this book can be defined privatively, but that is not enough. If this book is not about science popularizing at the philosophical or the nerdy level, what it *is* about is science popularization at the level of the universal and the everyday. Here the grab is sought in the quotidian anxieties, challenges, failures, and blissful moments immediately recognized by everyone—from the search for self-confidence to the experience of wonder at the immensity of the starry sky above. What unifies the chapters in this book, then, is a new deployment, specifically in the realm of science exposition, of the standard folklorist's creed: that the everyday world—the one in which most of us live most of the time—is full of richness, variety, and creativity. My claim is that attempts at science exposition at this level invariably draw in folkloric genres, strategies, or idioms that are already geared to it. This book contains ten chapters, each of which is an essay exploring an instance of science popularization that operates at, or is rooted in, the quotidian round. The instances are very diverse, and since each essay is shaped in response to the particular topic, so are the essays. Because they deal with popularizing strategies that can be brought to the surface quite directly, the first five essays are fairly short. The strategies analyzed in the remaining five essays require more probing and, in some cases, historical contextualization; hence these chapters are longer.

Quantitative analysis is a hallmark of science, and the first step is measurement, which presents special problems for the realms we most entrust to science: the very large and the very small. If the challenge for scientists is to develop instruments capable of such measurement, the challenge for science popularizers is to keep those magnitudes tied to everyday experience, which, impelled by everyday needs as computed in familiar scales, is similarly full of calculations of size, extent, and relative value. The problem, in other words, is that of relating the astro- and the nano- to finger-arithmetic. Starting with a souvenir brochure from Hoover Dam, I explore in chapter 1, "Formulas of Conversion," a set of stock expressions tapped often in discussions of monumental architecture, signaled by the formula "that's enough X to Y" (for example, "enough concrete . . . to build a 4-foot-wide sidewalk around the Earth at the Equator").[2] I pursue the formula in two opposite directions. On one hand, I suggest that the strategy has folk roots in the rough-and-ready, yet highly artistic, conversion formulas at the center of many proverbs: "a bird in the hand is worth two in the bush," "an ounce of prevention is worth a pound of cure," or "a picture is worth a thousand words" (the last example famously analyzed by Wolfgang Mieder [2004a]). In the other direction, I pursue the formula's progressive elaboration until it reaches realms of science popularizing that might be termed elite.

Many forms of religion and traditional wisdom offer models, regimens, and other practical guidance to individuals on how to achieve internal coherence, self-control, and self-direction. In chapter 2, "Leonardo and Copernicus at Aspen," I explore a modern variation on such practical guidance, specifically, the invocation of science heroes such as Leonardo da Vinci as personal role models in self-help books by motivational speaker Michael Gelb (1998, 2002). The same heroes tapped by elite popular science writers to elaborate the heroic story of science are tapped by Gelb in strategies that recall the traditional religious sermon, the folk-religious hagiography of the "patron saint," and conjurations of sympathetic magic. Gelb's final goal here is not the promotion of scientific understanding but the improvement of self-esteem, personal effectiveness, and corporate performance in the economic sphere.

The third chapter, "Opening the Two Totes," carries in another direction one of the concerns of chapter 2, specifically, the modern form of ritual known as the conference. I compare impressions of two mega-conferences that might be seen as contemporary popularizations of the spirit of *mythos* and *logos*: one hosted by the Mythic Imagination Institute, the other by the Committee for Skeptical Inquiry (CSI), publishers of *Skeptical Inquirer* magazine. The former organization invokes "myth" as our salvation, the latter as our downfall; both, while having some academic input, are mainly populated by non-academics from various ways of life who are concerned about the drift of the contemporary worldview. I encountered at the CSI conference two mother-daughter pairs, the mother in each case solicitously shepherding the daughter through the different presentations. The scene was familiar because I have experienced numerous instances of parents introducing their children to a place of worship and its culture, and yet it was startling because the scene in this case occurred within an organization that tends to pass harsh judgment on traditional religious belief. Here was the battle of *mythos* and *logos* enacted not at the academic seminar table but among parents working through the most basic of all cultural quandaries, the one with which Plato opens his discussion of myth in the *Republic*— namely, what stories should we tell our children?

If chapter 2 deals with conferences organized to improve the cultural climate by confronting assumptions that derail life and diminish human potential, chapter 3 deals with anxieties about a deeper—indeed, the ultimate—defect of life: the predicament traditionally designated "the problem of evil." The question of why there is evil in the world was a religious quandary before it became a topic of moral philosophy, and the reality of evil must have been a basic human experience as a condition for its becoming narrativized in religious mythology and then codified as a philosophical problem. In chapter 4, "Taking the Dawkins Challenge," I consider the

ways the concept of the "meme," born in a biological treatise on genet-
ics and Darwinian evolution but now a familiar pop-culture buzzword (or
meme), has been drawn into the problem of evil. Specifically, in some usages
"meme" merges with "virus" to connote the spread not of any idea but specifically of morally harmful ideas. I argue that this particular mutation of
the meme concept, by which Dawkins himself appears to be infected in
some of his more socially-politically polemical works, has been influenced
by a perspective (or "memeplex") that Dawkins stridently opposes—namely,
religious worldviews that locate the source of evil in invasive demons that
must be confronted through heroic free (and apparently meme-free) will.
This particular mutation of the meme is thus of significance to folklorists
primarily through its resonance with folk-religious ideas concerning the origin of evil; but it is also relevant to the traditional folkloristic interest in the
dissemination of traditional motifs and forms. Jack Zipes's (2006) theory of
the evolution of the folktale genre, which I critique in this chapter, explicitly
taps meme theory in confronting both the persistence of folklore forms and
the problem of evil.

Issues from the previous three chapters—self-direction and self-control,
anxieties about the prevailing worldview, living amid bad memes—converge
in chapter 5, "The Biggest Losers." Here I bring together two kinds or levels
of mythology: the "high" mythology of the grand cosmogonic story, on one
hand, and, on the other, the "low" mythology of unexamined everyday ideology and habit—the latter as exposed most famously by Roland Barthes in
his modern classic, *Mythologies* (1995). I consider arguments made by Joel
Primack and Nancy Ellen Abrams (2006; Abrams and Primack 2011), a
physicist and public-policy attorney husband-wife team. They are troubled
by the fact that science is popularly perceived as asking the public to give up
the anthropocentric notion of cosmos as home—leaving us, in effect, alien-
ated from the cosmos. As a remedy, Primack and Abrams argue that modern
cosmology offers scientifically grounded substitutes for our old anthropocentric cravings; for example, although we are not the spatial center, we can
still legitimately view ourselves as occurring at the center of cosmic time. In
addition, they suggest ways in which varied and colorful mythico-religious
imagery can be selectively salvaged and re-purposed in the presentation of
science. Through such measures, they claim, we can retain the grand cosmogonic story, with ourselves at the center.

An earlier wave of popular science writers, led by Steven Weinberg, had
called for heroic, stoic acceptance of Copernican de-centering, but Primack
and Abrams preach instead a search for substitute ways to satisfy our anthropocentric cravings. I argue that this high-mythology shift parallels a shift

that has taken place in the (Barthesian) low mythology of the same period, evident especially in the marketing of popular diet plans: from heroic "no pain, no gain" regimes to more moderate methods of appetite control based on colorful, texture-y, "sensible" substitutes of lighter (that is, "lite") nutritional fare. In what is perhaps a broader shift of worldview, strategies for controlling our lofty cosmic yearnings thus resonate intriguingly with broadly circulating low mythologies arising around the everyday problem of reining in our personal girth. This microcosm-macrocosm parallel newly inflects a very old mythological conceit, one that assumes there are formal and/or functional sympathies between the universe and the human body.

Chapter 6, "It's a Wonderfully Conflicted Life," examines four science films made in the late 1950s and early 1960s by Hollywood director Frank Capra: *Our Mr. Sun, Hemo the Magnificent, The Unchained Goddess,* and *The Strange Case of the Cosmic Rays.* With the prophetic motto "education through entertainment," these films were a staple of grade-school science education (with reportedly 1,600 copies of each film in circulation). The films recycled the formulas, gimmicks, and populist sentiment of Capra's earlier films (including *It's a Wonderful Life, Lost Horizon,* and *Mr. Smith Goes to Washington*). At the heart of Capra's filmic argument is the conflict between science and religion, and much has been made of the subtle and unsubtle strategies he taps in these films to present science and religion as compatible. By contrast, I argue that not two but three entities are juxtaposed in these films—science, religion, and mythology—and that mythology "takes the fall" for religion by, in effect, representing the parts of religion that cannot be harmonized with science. The mythology Capra creates, through the new form of animism known as animation, presages the sort of archaico-modernistic superhero fare now common in children's television. I explore the films as a twentieth-century popularization of attitudes toward religion, superstition, idolatry, and mythology that developed during the eighteenth-century philosophical Enlightenment and were carried into the nineteenth century by the very thinkers who (however inadequately) made folklore an object of social analysis. Indeed, Capra's triad of mythology, religion, and science is none other than E. B. Tylor's three grand evolutionary stages of Savagery, Barbarism, and Civilization. With the "Ode to Joy" from Beethoven's Ninth Symphony as recurrent musical background, Capra's science films all conclude with triumphant visions of science, its origins and growth, and its promise for humanity—thus adding a scientific stamp to the populist optimism that is Capra's cinematic signature.

Popular science, in fact, often works by offering stirring visions to the reader-viewer, and in the next chapter I explore other cosmic visions offered in the name of science—in this case, visions inspired less by the heroic story of science than by momentary, personal epiphanies concerning the human place in the cosmos. In chapter 7, "Departures from Earth I," I consider a moment of sublimity conjured by Carl Sagan around a photograph of the Earth taken from the edge of the solar system by the *Voyager* space probe. I juxtapose Sagan's cosmic epiphany with a parallel moment described by Garrison Keillor in one of his Lake Wobegon monologues. Keillor similarly attributes his own cosmic vision to a departure from earth, but of a more humble sort: a Ferris wheel ride at the state fair. Sagan's vision is portentous, elaborate, and loquacious, while Keillor's is personal and set out in local-color plain speech—his monologues amounting to literarily honed personal experience narratives (on this genre, see Dolby Stahl [1989]). But otherwise Sagan and Keillor offer, point for point, the same vision. Sagan presents his vision as though it were made possible by science. But by juxtaposing Sagan's epiphany with Keillor's and with other literary renditions of small-town cosmic visions, I present an alternative take in which Sagan's vision emerges as a tweaking of a cosmic epiphany rooted in human cognition and culture in general rather than as a possibility opened by science. To put it differently, I explore the folk roots of Sagan's high-tech epiphany.

But not all is harmony in the cosmos. To exemplify the converse—the moment of literarily created cosmic disharmony—I analyze in chapter 8, "Departures from Earth II," an article written for the *Atlantic Monthly* by ace disaster writer William Langewiesche about the tragedy of the space shuttle *Columbia*, emphasizing the ways he conjures, through excursions into the physics and engineering behind space flight, a sense of not just human but also cosmic conflict and pathos. His middle-brow treatise, energized by the appeal of astronauts as national heroes, draws upon popular genres ranging from detective novels to the biblical story of Genesis. Scientific visions of cosmic disharmony, like those of harmony, are developed out of literary traditions with folk-religious roots.

Continuing in somewhat different stride with the theme of astronauts and space exploration, chapter 9, "Goodbye Spoony Juney Moon," presents the analysis of Tom Stoppard's play *Jumpers* discussed above. Stoppard's play is a multi-ring circus in which cosmic quandaries pursued through space exploration and mathematical paradoxes are juxtaposed with a pulpy scenario of crime investigation and a failing marriage. To this theatrical circus I bring a method of analysis developed originally around a traditional mythic story told by the Tsimshian people of the Northwest Coast of North America. The method was developed by anthropologist Claude Lévi-Strauss, whose career parallels Stoppard's. Asking why a method that seems to reveal something about a Tsimshian traditional myth should also do so for a modern science-infused theatrical farce, I explore the relationship among myth, ritual, and popular theater.

The tenth and final chapter, "Is Lucretius a God," considers the first-century BCE Roman poet Lucretius's epic *De Rerum Natura*, a landmark work of ancient science that remained influential as science through the Renaissance (nowadays it is more often read as literature). I argue that *De Rerum Natura* is not just an example of ancient science but also of ancient popular science. My focus is Lucretius's strategies for convincing readers of the validity of materialistic atomism, especially his master plan of teaching and glorifying the new form of understanding by promoting it through the traditional genre of epic—replete with poetic meter, heroes, gods, ship-wrecks, and invocations of the Muses. Like most epics, *De Rerum Natura* is set within a mythological cosmos—the worldview that the new atomistic understanding will directly challenge. Lucretius's marvelous text is in fact one folkloric form employed to defeat others: specifically, epic—a genre that celebrates heroic human striving—employed to dislodge the assumptions that inhere in mythology and superstition or, as it is now termed, folk belief. The latter for Lucretius is epitomized in the supposition, in the story of Iphigeneia, that the sacrifice of this woman will enable the Greeks to voyage to Troy (Lucretius 1994:12 [80–102]).

Lucretius mythologizes in the service of demythologizing and in doing so largely adumbrates the basic strategies of persuasion popular science writers still adopt today. I develop this claim by revisiting the elite writers I treated in my earlier book and comparing their basic strategies to those of Lucretius. Although Lucretius lived in the era of "bread and circuses" (the phrase is from Juvenal), Lucretius himself in some respects would have to be categorized as elite. Certainly, his work was aimed at the literate minority of his time; moreover, the contemporary writers to whom I compare him form an elite (in the sense discussed above). However, in this chapter I do not (as I did in my earlier book) explore the larger, more complex arguments of the contemporary writers in question—of a sort that would be pursued by the "true believers" of popular science literature. Rather, I focus on their most basic and durable hooks and gimmicks, under the assumption that strategies hearty enough to call for comparison over a two-millennia span will tend toward universal popular appeal. Finally, regarding my earlier observations on the greater transparency of strategy in mass (over elite) popular science, we find in Lucretius a particularly candid depiction of one of the most persistent strategies of science popularizing in the face of anticipated reluctance from the audience; namely, science seduction through art:

My art is not without a purpose. Physicians, when they wish to treat children with a nasty dose of wormwood, first smear the rim of the cup with
the sweet yellow fluid of honey . . .

In the same way our doctrine often seems unpalatable to those who
have not handled it, and the masses shrink from it. That is why I have tried
to administer my philosophy to you in the dulcet strains of poesy, to touch
it with the sweet honey of the Muses. (ibid.:32–33 [1.926–58])

Distantly anachronistic comparison is methodologically treacherous.
Nonetheless, I will argue that when one has isolated the expressive and per-
suasive strategies that link popular science writers of today with the roman
epic poet Lucretius of the first century BCE, one will also sense the affin-
ity of these strategies with the expressive forms that have always interested
folklorists. The thought that it's all been done before is both intriguing and
troubling: what does it mean that such a prescient summation of our present situation was set out by an epic bard two millennia ago? Perhaps the
disconnection between the state of knowledge (or that part of knowledge we
now call science) and lived experience simply must be accepted from here
on out as part of the human condition—but a part toward which traditional
folkloric genres and forms of expression will continue to play an active,
domesticating role.

***

Before closing this introduction, I would like to add a further note
about the relation of *Science, Bread, and Circuses* (*SB&C*) to the book that
preceded it, *The Ancient Mythology of Modern Science* (*AMMS*). While
Science, Bread, and Circuses, as noted, is complete in itself, one who chooses
to read the two books as a pair will encounter a smattering of examples
considered in the first book and then reconsidered, in a different context,
in this one. The reconsideration in this book will always involve a shift
toward the "mass" end of the audience spectrum; through such shifts the
reader will catch a glimpse of the different levels at which science exposition can be pitched. For example, in popular science there is no emblem
of science, its demands, and its payoff more persistent and powerful than
the idea of the Copernican revolution. In *AMMS* I consider this hallowed
emblem as used by elite popular science writers to tell the heroic story of
science and as a symbol of the personal transformation that a commitment
to science demands. In *SB&C* the Copernican revolution reappears in two
contexts, both of which lead not further into science but away from it. As
I describe in chapter 2 of *SB&C*, motivational speaker Michael Gelb also
invokes Copernicus as a symbol of personal transformation, but of a kind
disconnected from science and related instead to optimizing self-confidence

and personal performance. Tom Stoppard invokes the Copernican revolution as a sort of cosmic metaphor of shifts in public worldview taking place around him.

A second example involves the metaphor of the human mind as a society (made up of different brain functionaries: librarians, executives, facilitators, and so on). In *AMMS* I consider the use of this image as a heuristic metaphor in recent elite popular science about artificial intelligence research (emphasizing books by Marvin Minsky and Daniel Dennett), while in *SB&C* I consider its use by Frank Capra, through studio animation, to convey the brain biology of his time to the broadest possible television audience. Other than my own commentaries here and in *AMMS*, I know of no instance of these two levels or forms of science popularization, rooted in the same metaphor, being brought into the same discussion; and I suspect that bringing them together will not meet with an entirely sympathetic response from the elite realm. That absence confirms the reality of different kinds and levels of science popularization that proceed, in some instances at least, in relative autonomy from one another. In sum, through these and a smattering of other examples, one who chooses to read the books as a pair will learn something about the variety of science popularizations. This variety consists in part of the diversity of illustrations but also, and perhaps more interesting, of the same illustrations refashioned in different ways toward different levels of culture, audience, and human experience.

***

The relationship of science and folklore should be—indeed, I believe already is, implicitly—at the very center of folkloristic inquiry. For the claimed authority of science forms the single most potent theme in the idea of modernity, an idea that more than any other has engendered and propelled the idea of folklore (mostly as antithesis and/or nemesis). There are, all folklorists know, many contending definitions of folklore; but the historically deepest and most resonant of these spring from, and give expression to, concern for the life of traditional expressive forms in a world that proclaims itself fundamentally changed and no longer in need of them. The challenges to that proclaimed new world are many. Most famously, Bruno Latour, in *We Have Never Been Modern* (1993), points to elite journalists' relentless insistence on the mixing of science and non-science, for example, and asserts that the new world is non-attainable or at least not yet attained. Richard Bauman and Charles Briggs (2003) carry Latour's critique into sociolinguistic theory, and through it into traditional expressive forms, by asking whether such theories escape the parochialism they conjure as their foil. A number of folkloristic works—Diane Goldstein's *Once upon a Virus*

(2004), for example—spring not so much from a criticism or critique of scientific language or method as from an insistence that speakers of this language will succeed in bettering the human condition only if they are willing to acknowledge vernacular ways of understanding and dealing with disease and proposed cures. My work is in sympathy with all of these works and others but focuses on what seems to me the most direct encounter possible between folklore and science; namely, attempts—meeting with results from silly to sublime—to rephrase and thus domesticate scientific findings and claims in folklorically imbued popular forms.

NOTES

1. It is in part the breadth of expressive genres considered in this book that leads me to identify myself as a folklorist in this title, as compared with my previous book, in which I identified myself through my genre specialty—that is, as a mythologist. In the context of oral expressive forms, folklore is generally the broader term (though there are exceptions; e.g., in Boasian tradition, "myth" sometimes meant a group's oral narrative stock generally). The fact that I identified myself as a mythologist in the previous book has to do with one other factor central to that book but only peripheral to this one. That is, contemporary elite popular science writers often invoke "myth" (either the term or specific examples from mythology) as a foil, against which they claim to demonstrate the superiority of science. This rhetorical tradition is an old one, practiced by philosophers from the earliest times before being taken up by scientists (cf. Brisson 2004). Part of my aim in *AMMS* in identifying myself as a mythologist was polemical, for one of my goals was to show that popular science writers practice the same forms of analysis and persuasion they point to pejoratively in mythology.

2. As I write this, a television commercial is airing that appeals to public eco-consciousness by offering a home water-filtration system and pointing out that each year Americans use enough plastic bottles to reach around the world 190 times at the Equator.

1

Formulas of Conversion
A Proverbial Approach to Astronomic Magnitudes

Finally, there it is.[1] Despite its monumental proportions, you approach it from above as the blast-furnace heat calls to mind Dante's descent through the rings of Hell. It claimed ninety-six human lives. With the Great Depression and lean war years in recent memory, my parents' low-budget honeymoon trip was a sort of early post–New Deal pilgrimage to see and, as attested by some fading photos, to stand on this symbol of hope. They purchased a Navajo blanket nearby. I do not recall the Navajo blanket ever wrapped around me, but I do recall it being draped each night, for the first few months anyway, over our first television set—a monstrous Packard Bell monitor about the size of a piano—when that mysterious new technology first appeared in our corner of the world. There is something poetic here: the latest magic object of rapidly advancing technology shrouded in a gift of ancient technology, namely, the loom.

I seized an opportunity to see *Hoover Dam* for myself a few summers ago, this particular infernal descent driven by nostalgia but also by serious scholarly motives. For I saw an opportunity to test a hypothesis that had been kicking around in the back of my head for years but which I had yet to write down. The hypothesis is that large-scale, publicly funded engineering projects inevitability give rise to proverbial sayings, or something like proverbial sayings, of this form:

$X = Y$

or $X \geq Y$

where X is an abstract and/or unfamiliar quantity or measure and Y is a familiar or concrete quantity or measure (very appropriate term in this case, "concrete").

Within this formula one encounters recurrent patterns, especially the phrase "that's enough to" and, in the case of linear dimensions, the

DOI: 10.7330/9780874219708.c001

phrase "if laid end-to-end"; "football fields" is a noticeably recurrent unit of measure.

Immediately, I found confirmation of my hypothesis in the official *Hoover Dam Souvenir Guide* (2003), on the back page in a section titled "Tell 'em back home," which, given that home for academics means working on books, is what I am doing now. According to the brochure, I am supposed to convey eight factoids. Five of these, indeed the first five of the eight, are formulas of conversion of the type I just described; within these five we have three "that's enough tos" and one "end-to-end." Such formulas also arise in popular science writing, where they can be fairly complex (I present an example later), but those we encounter in public construction projects are rather vaudevillian—intellectual corndogs, if you will. Here they are:

> Hoover Dam contains "enough concrete . . . to build a four-foot-wide sidewalk around the Earth at the Equator" ("at the Equator" seems also to be an invariant part of this rather standard formula).
>
> "During peak electricity periods, enough water runs through the generators to fill 14 average-sized swimming pools . . . in 3 seconds."
>
> Its reservoir "contains enough water to cover the entire state of Pennsylvania with 1 ft. of water."
>
> At its base, it is "as thick . . . as two football fields measured end-to-end."

The remaining point, actually number one in the brochure, intentionally or not reflects the eastern- vs. western-US appropriations battles that surrounded the construction of this dam: even though situated below ground level, Hoover Dam nevertheless is "171 feet taller than the Washington Monument." I briefly note that points six and seven of the Hoover Dam brochure are also of direct folkloric interest, though of a different kind. Point six, which I alluded to in my opening remarks, states: "96 men were killed in industrial accidents at the dam. None were buried in the concrete."

The last bit is almost certainly a reference to another inevitable spinoff, for legends of workers buried in the cement show up at virtually every monumental construction site. The legend may be a modern variant on the ancient motif Stith Thompson (1955–58) labeled "Foundation Sacrifice" (S261), itself perhaps a manifestation of a primordial anthropocentrism, an insistence that anything in the cosmos ultimately derives its power to hold together from us. These deaths mark the limit of where formulas of conversion can be applied, perhaps again out of anthropocentric conceit; for to have followed the ninety-six deaths with "that's enough men, laid end-to-end, to . . ." would certainly have been perceived as a morally callous application of a mathematical calculus.

The seventh point in the brochure is the inevitable bit of pop totemism that similarly accompanies monumental construction, an obligatory juxtaposing of the gargantuan and the cute: we are informed about a dog mascot of the construction workers, buried near the entrance to the visitor center. Perhaps the dog is a substitute foundation sacrifice. If so, a superstitious person might wonder whether this substitution explains the fact that some of the great Works Progress Administration (WPA) dams in recent years have begun to leak.

Such formulas of conversion might occur in any realm in which our ordinary, everyday experience of quantitative measures fails. It is not that we are unable to intellectually register a measure of a quantity but that we are unable to conjure a *feeling* of that quantity. In the case of human engineering, this means the more extreme regions of the monumental and the miniature; in science, astronomical and microscopic scales, such as the micro-chip and nano-world. In the organic realm, such formulas often appear as imagined unraveling of organic structures that are fractal in design or, in their natural state, all wadded up: DNA, intestines, capillaries, that sort of thing.

The main reason for linking such formulas to scholarship on proverbs is found in the nature of traditional proverbs. Specifically, underneath the idea of conversion lies an assertion of some sort of equivalence. Note how many well-known proverbs are assertions of equivalence, often with connotations of convertibility or "exchange value":

Example 1: An Ounce of Prevention Is Worth a Pound of Cure

1 oz. P = 16 oz. C

In American society we recognize two main systems of measures: everyday (quarts, pounds, miles) and metric. The first indexes, and indeed many of its units originated from, practical household quantities; metric measures, by contrast, index the scientific. Rule-of-thumb, everyday prevention and cure would sound stilted were we to convert it to metrics (i.e., grams of prevention and cure), implying a quantitative precision that isn't there.

Example 2A: A Bird in the Hand Is Worth Two in the Bush

$B_{hand} = 2 \, B_{bush}$

Example 2B: A Stitch in Time Saves Nine

$S_{it} = 9_{-it}$

2A and 2B offer the same formula—a formula that relegates any intrinsic value of things to control of them—directed respectively to hunting and clothes-making, two complementary domains of archaic economies. It is a commonplace that many proverbs function to orient us to the world. Even when obscure and multiply interpretable, they set us up for decision making, sometimes, as in these cases, within an economics of efficiency.

Example 3: A Picture Is Worth a Thousand Words

$P = 10^3 \, W$

Wolfgang Mieder (2004a) did a fascinating presentation on this formula at the American Folklore Society annual meeting,[2] detailing the many variations it has undergone, particularly in popular cultural realms and especially as an advertising jingle. In processes of creation and dissemination, the formulas of conversion I focus on are like this advertising formula; they are recently minted marketing content in traditional form, aka "fakelore" in Richard Dorson's famous formula (which he later softened).

One other way formulas of conversion differ from the traditional proverb is that they do not proffer directly useful, practical advice. But consider this: along with those traditional proverbs that assert equivalence and convertibility, there is another set of rather metaphysically inclined traditional proverbs that articulate limits of convertibility:

Example 4: You Can't Make a Silk Purse from a Sow's Ear

$SE \neq SP$

Example 5: You Can't Squeeze Blood from a Turnip

$T \neq B$

Example 6: Don't Make a Mountain out of a Molehill

$Mol \neq Mt$

The last one especially has to do with maintaining a workable sense of perspective. Such formulas do offer advice of a more abstract kind, and that is what the formulas of conversion I am discussing try to do: give us a sense of perspective by translating quantities we cannot envision to ones we can, thus keeping us *on scale*.

Time and space are particularly common but by no means the only possible foci for formulas of conversion. Some invoke a microcosmic/macrocosmic relation, such as that between a family-domestic economy and the national economy. Everyone has heard the sentiment regarding the size of the national economy: "A billion here, a billion there, pretty soon you're talking real money." In the opposite direction, I recently heard an analyst proclaim (and I hope that either I misheard or that he was math-challenged) that every family's share of the national debt is now $450,000. The highly abstract business of probability and its practical dimension of risk management are also common, and a standard baseline is the probability of being killed in an airplane crash (though being struck by lightning is also common). For example, some popular scientific literature I recently received proclaims:[3]

> The chance of being killed by an asteroid is about one in 5,000, greater than that of being killed in a plane crash.

It goes on to explain that

> this is because an asteroid strike could kill millions, whereas in a plane crash, the numbers are small. No one has been hit in 1,000 years.

As if to alarm, to get you to purchase more factoids, it offers another formula:

> More people work in a single McDonald's restaurant than are employed worldwide to monitor asteroids.

Another interesting comparison would be the likelihood of death from asteroids and death from fast food.

Folkloristic studies of the proverb have centered on form, variation, and function—all of which are relevant to these formulas of conversion. But other realms of scholarly inquiry are also relevant to the analysis of such formulas. The first is a possible historical dimension. These examples are secular, but historical precedents are found in the religious sphere, if only because religion is a locus for oversize issues: creation, the size of the cosmos, the end of time. I will mention one example I heard in the context of Catholic grade-school religion class and which I have since encountered in writings of early Christian writers, suggesting that it is at least two millennia old. The scenario is one designed to dramatize the concept of eternity; common to the variants is a yearly cyclic repetition of some minute but incremental act. The variant I heard is that the nun who sweeps the church is instructed to leave one more grain of dust unswept each year until the church is full of dust—and even then, it was said, the big E is just beginning.

$$E > CF \times DY$$
where CF is a church-full and DY is a dust-year

The next three possible scholarly angles on such formulas all fit somewhere under the realm of "cognition."

The first of these concerns the issue of cognitive forms in scientific vs. so-called folk knowledge; for "folk" is a standard term used by academic specialists, in phrases such as "folk psychology," to designate what is, or is imagined to be, the way the world is understood in everyday terms by nonspecialists. Ever since Plato juxtaposed expressions of skepticism toward myth to his advocacy of philosophy—a kind of pursuit rooted in the logic of propositions—there has been some tendency to regard narrative or story as the vehicle of folk knowledge and as a second fiddle, a cognitive vehicle less precise and less powerful than logical analytical reason working through propositions. There is much to object to in this idea, but even if we were to accept it, proverbs would give us pause. For clearly, proverbs are a genre of folk knowledge, and their format is that favored by philosophy and science, namely, the proposition: a straightforward subject followed by a predicate.

One of the most fascinating works on the proverb, without intending to be so, is Max Weber's (1958, especially pp. 48–50) classic book *The Protestant Ethic and the Spirit of Capitalism.* In this work, Weber announces that his orienting concept will be the nebulous, cloudy, all-penetrating substance of "spirit"—as in the "spirit of capitalism"; elsewhere he uses the term *worldview.* When he turns to actually describing the "spirit" or "worldview" of capitalism, the very first thing Weber gives us is a terse proverbial formula that forms the quintessential expression—we might think of it as the E = MC^2—of the capitalist worldview, namely:

> *Time* Is Money
>
> $T = M$

We have here a kind of popular knowledge, propositional in form, that, like the scientific equation, aspires to a summarizing elegance—and to asserting a convertibility if not exactly of energy and matter, then of quanta at least vaguely reminiscent of these, namely, of industriousness and capital accumulation.

Another relevant scholarly focus would be the recent wave of interest in so-called embodied reason, promoted by George Lakoff, Mark Johnson, and their many followers (Lakoff and Johnson 1999). The connection of this focus to formulas of conversion would seem obvious, for in many cases the x = y amounts to the conversion of disembodied measurements of quantity into embodied ones. It is not that one has necessarily had the experience of wading through a Pennsylvania that is a foot deep in water but rather that one can put together the experience of the length of Pennsylvania—perhaps from driving through it or at least seeing it on a map and comparing its map size to other states one has driven through—with that of wading in foot-deep water. Lakoff and Johnson argue that even the cognitive forms that give us our most abstract knowledge claims derive from bodily experience. For example, the very possibility of identifying a "category" or "set" (of anything) derives from the experience of the body as container, so that some things are in it while others are outside, thus demarcating a "set." If one accepts that theory of the origin of abstract knowledge, then formulas of conversion provide methods not so much of embodying but of *re-embodying* knowledge; they raise all sorts of issues regarding the classic problem of the relation of the abstract and, again, the concrete.

Third, one should consider a long-running object of fascination in linguistics, namely, the seeming human capacity to hold together and ultimately unravel so-called linguistic embedding, as in this sentence taken from a book about language by Steven Pinker (1995:204–7): "The guy who is sitting between the table that I like and the empty chair just winked."

The basic sentence is "The guy just winked." Embedded in it is "The guy is sitting between the table and the empty chair"; and embedded in that is "I like the table" or possibly "I like the guy." But according to Pinker, we cannot process the following equally grammatical sentence: "The rapidity that the motion that the wing that the hummingbird has has has is remarkable."

Not even my computer can process this sentence, for it has underlined in red the second and third "has." Pinker speculates that what differentiates the two sentences is that the former embeds different kinds of phrases, while the latter's embedding is *merely recursive*. What is confusing is "keeping a particular kind of phrase in memory, intending to get back to it, at the same time as . . . analyzing another example of *that very same kind of phrase*."[4]

Although I suspect that Pinker's (ibid.) theory may be wrong in some details, I am inspired to suggest an admittedly loose analogy in the realm of quantitative understanding. Exponential notation or so-called scientific notation—basically a terse means to add zeros to an integer—is a powerful but strictly recursive device in formal mathematics. Like the hummingbird sentence, we can parse exponential notation intellectually as we learn in algebra and chemistry, but we cannot, or at least normally do not, process exponential notation in the quantitative sensibility of everyday life. It marks one of those points at which higher-level math disconnects from everyday senses of quantity, those we intuitively feel.

At this point I turn to an example of a work of popular science exposition that deals with the size of the universe. Rather than present the standard recursive operation of scientific exponential notation, this work attempts to convey astronomical quantities through a strategy of embedding that is tangible and variegated. Edward Packard's (1994) *Imagining the Universe: A Visual Journey* attempts to convey the size of the very large through a series of shrinkings, each followed by a refocusing and an accompanying map or diagram.[5]

The first shrinking is of the Earth until it fits inside Candlestick Park near San Francisco Bay, displayed through a map on the cover of the book. With the entire cosmos adjusted to the scale of the Earth inside the ballpark, the moon would be across the bay near Oakland International Airport, Venus would be near El Paso, and Jupiter and Saturn would still be out in space.

Then Packard shrinks the Earth to the size of a baseball, "floating over home plate in Candlestick Park" (ibid.:18). At this point the solar system is still bigger than the Bay area. The Earth is again shrunk, until a "grain-of-sand-sized Earth" (ibid.:28) floats over home plate. The sun is now the size of a golf ball.

Next the sun is shrunk to a grain of sand floating over home plate; then, after more refocusings, finally the solar system itself is shrunk to a grain of sand floating over home plate. At this point, "Our galaxy, the Milky Way, consisting of hundreds of billions of stars, covers part of San Francisco (including Candlestick Park) and extends across San Francisco Bay . . . Each dot in the pages that follow represents not a star, or even a galaxy, but a cluster of galaxies" (ibid.:62).

After eight mostly blank pages, we arrive—like the dart thrower imagined by Lucretius (1994) millennia ago[6]—at the edge of our universe; but, in a scenario of curved space-time unlike anything Lucretius ever imagined, "we may discover that we have returned to our microscopic Earth, deep inside the grain-of-sand–sized solar system floating over home plate in San Francisco" (ibid.:68).

Several points in this little exercise are of interest here from a folkloristic point of view. They include *repeating formulas*, especially of units of measure, where instead of light years we have baseballs and golf balls, grains of sand, baseball parks, and the size of the Bay area and the Earth. The refrain "floating over home plate" is like the phrase "that lives in the house that Jack built" or the phrase "and all for the want of a nail" of familiar ditties.[7] Such phrases offer fixed points within series of embedded refocusings. Also, I believe I have detected a mistake: following the pattern established by Packard himself, the last of his formulas quoted above should have ended "home plate in Candlestick Park," not "home plate in San Francisco." Such "mistakes" are common in, and arguably part of the charm of, incremental theme-and-variation folkloric performances; in this case, the propensity to err might easily have been compounded by a topic—namely, cosmic immensity—that could easily cause one to lose one's moorings.

In considering Packard's (1994) baseball strategy, a folklorist might also note that athletics and athletic playing fields are among the most recurrent images in the assertion of microcosmic-macrocosmic parallels in mythological cosmologies. For example, in some Native American cosmologies, the shape and fate of the cosmos seem directly tied to the nature and fate of ritually played athletic contests set in the center of sacred space or architecture. For whatever reason, long before Packard's little book and long before the advent of modern science, the athletic field was a potent image for attempting to envision the cosmos.

The figuration of the universe in Packard's book is also tied to various kinds of motor activities. Some of these are imagined in the form of the athletic microcosm; for example, when the grain-of-sand *Earth* floats over home plate, "Venus is . . . in the catcher's mitt . . . Jupiter . . . [is] three quarters of the way to the mound . . . Saturn . . . near first base . . . [and] Pluto is a speck of dust near the center-field wall" (ibid.: 28). Venus in the catcher's mitt: a nice mythological turnaround since this goddess has us all in her mitt. Then there is the flipping of pages, an activity that itself conveys a different but familiar everyday experience of distance.

We thus have multiply overlaid or embedded schemes, tied to diverse mental and motor activities; and, to the extent that we can mentally retain one while embarking on the next, these are to cumulative effect. All of this is highly inefficient, certainly as compared to exponential notation of the size of the cosmos. But, like the football fields end to end at the base of Hoover Dam, such strategies may succeed in conveying more of a *feeling* of that size than does exponential notation.

One finds many such strategies of tangible, quantitative embedding in traditional mythological cosmologies and cosmogonies. The Oceanic cosmologies that I work with, for example, overlay multiple temporal and spatial domains. And the whole of the duration of the cosmos is finally mapped onto yet another form of experienced quantity, that of real-time duration, when such accounts are performed as long chants; sometimes they seem interminably long. Considered in the light of such examples, Packard's little book might be seen as an attempt to re-mythologize and re-embody the cosmos of exponential notation.

The human mind may not be particularly well structured to do what such formulas of conversion attempt. We seem to be equipped with, or able to quickly develop, an everyday sense of quantity. We also seem to have, though in varying degrees, an ability to do abstract mathematics of quantities that never touch the ground. Each project has its integrity. The attempt to connect these projects to one another seems to me less natural, more in need of contrivance, than either is in itself. A big mystery is why making such connections is important to anyone. Perhaps the source is once again anthropocentric, a hubris that refuses to accept that there could be a gap between what we are equipped to sense or feel and what is.

In his famous television series *Cosmos* (2000), Carl Sagan discusses exponential notation through the quantities known as "googol" (10 to the 100th power) and "googolplex" (10 to the power of googol); the former is a quantity much larger than the total number of ultimate particles in the accessible universe, and the latter is many times larger still.[8] As the scene progresses, Sagan starts to write out, on what appears to be a roll of cash-register tape, a googolplex, one zero after another. We soon see the roll of zero-filled tape lying across a table in a dining hall at Cambridge University, then Sagan further unrolling the tape as he walks purposefully across the campus, traversing time as well as space through the hallowed ground's association with Isaac Newton. He finally pronounces this exercise "spectacularly futile" and points out that a piece of paper large enough to contain all the zeros of a googolplex "couldn't be stuffed into the known universe." Everyday hubris is clearly defeated; yet the episode goes on to suggest an interesting turnaround, for if the universe effortlessly transcends our *everyday* measures of quantity, *scientific* measures can effortlessly transcend the universe. The inadequate piece of paper, in the end, is made adequate by the triumph of higher-level mathematics. For a googolplex, Sagan shows us, can be written quite simply as:

$$10^{10^{100}}$$

Whether confronting the astronomic magnitudes of the physical universe or of the mathematics designed to deal with it, one cannot help but feel that everydayness has been abandoned. In reviewing a conference he attended on contemporary scientific cosmology, literary writer John Updike (2000:586) closed with a hunter-gatherer's exasperated lament: "Even in cosmology," he says, "billions should count for something."

NOTES

1. This chapter stems from a talk I delivered at the annual meeting of the Hoosier Folklore Society, November 12, 2004, Terre Haute, Indiana.

2. See Mieder (2004b) for the published version and also Dundes's (1994:46) comments on the "finite number of proverb compositional or architectural formulas."

3. The factoids considered here are taken from "Card 18" of a set of cards (foldout pages designed for a loose-leaf folder) I received in a mail promotion for a subscription to a series of such cards with a registered trademark "Secrets of the Universe." The material is identified as produced under license to International Masters Publishers, with a copyright date of MCMXCIX and a mail-order address in Pittsburgh.

4. Following Pinker, the basic sentence is "The rapidity that the motion has is remarkable." Embedded in this are the sentence "The motion that the wing has is remarkable" and the phrase "the wing that the hummingbird has."

5. For the series of shrinkings considered here, see the first part of Packard (1994:5–69). In the second part of his book, Packard offers a reciprocal journey to the very small, the first step of which consists of expanding a baseball to the size of a baseball park. Two other recent popular science works built around rough-and-ready scientific analogies, quantitative and qualitative, are Joel Levy (2011) and Weinstein and Adam (2008).

6. First-century BCE atomist Lucretius, in his poem *On the Nature of the Universe* (Lucretius 1994:33), portrays a dart thrower traveling to the edge of the universe to test whether it is finite or infinite. See the discussion of Lucretius in chapter 10.

7. In his popular book on "chaos theory," James Gleick (1987:23) invokes the "want of a nail" ditty amid a rumination on an issue that, in another way, poses the problem of the limits of calculability, namely, the potentially ramifying consequences of any event—the so-called butterfly effect.

8. The scene is from the episode "The Lives of the Stars" from *Cosmos* (2000).

2

Leonardo and Copernicus at Aspen
How Science Heroes Can Improve Your Bottom Line

Ironically, organizations everywhere are issuing urgent calls for greater creativity, innovation, and involvement from all levels. They ask their employees to "think out of the box" while confining them in boxes.

CHAPTER 1 CONSIDERED TRADITIONAL PROVERBIAL TEMPLATES that offer mechanisms for converting and thus comparatively assessing everyday values; but this is just one example from the myriad ways traditional folkloric and folk-religious forms function psychologically to help individuals achieve a sense of personal coherence, direction, and effectiveness.[1] The mechanisms are legion: epic heroes provide role models; sermons, revivals, festivals, and spectacles energize; rituals and pilgrimages walk participants through life strategies; games raise verbal and kinetic skills; techniques of prayer, meditation, and confession encourage self-assessment; and practices of the sort ethnographers label *magical* convey enlarged visions of an individual's ability to influence the cosmos—to mention a few more possibilities.

Under the rubrics of "self-help" and "motivational speaking" (the former associated more with an individual who is reading, the latter with a corporate audience that is listening), the last few decades have seen a florescence of secular versions of such traditional strategies of self-improvement. These new variants are secular in two main senses. First, their ultimate goal is success in a practical, inner-world sense, notably in work and human relationships (rather than, say, improved relationship with the gods or salvation in the form of eternal life). Second, the entities at the core of the appeal are not gods or divine media such as "grace" but rather psychological entities (admittedly elusive ones) such as "your inner self" or "your true potential." That said, the new forms of self-improvement borrow heavily from their

DOI: 10.7330/9780874219708.c002

traditional religious and folkloric forebears, as I illustrate below. Successful motivational and self-help speakers and writers often bear some sort of personal signature, a hook or gimmick identified uniquely with one particular approach to self-improvement. In this chapter I explore the writings of a motivational speaker and writer whose signature lies largely in an appeal to science and its heroes.

The epigraph that opens this chapter is taken from Michael Gelb's (1998:138) national bestseller *How to Think Like Leonardo da Vinci: Seven Steps to Genius Every Day*. This book was followed by *The How to Think Like Leonardo da Vinci Workbook* (Gelb 1999), which, when flipped over, becomes *The How to Think Like Leonardo da Vinci Notebook*, full of mostly empty pages to fill with your Leonardo-like thinking. The *Workbook/Notebook*, in turn, was followed by the more expansive and ecumenical *Discover Your Genius: How to Think Like History's Ten Most Revolutionary Minds* (Gelb 2002). These works are rooted in Gelb's motivational speaking, a world whose consummate expression is a secular sermon typically performed before businesspeople or administrators, often in places like Aspen. Such sermons easily metamorphose into published books typically shelved in or around the topic "self-help."

Indeed, in the brief passage with which I opened, one encounters—in the now-familiar imagery of boxes—what Sandra Dolby (2005:66) has said is "the ultimate message of all self-help books . . . that individuals must detach themselves from the conditioning imposed by the surrounding culture." Escaping from the box is the beginning of what Gelb promises the reader; his treatise is one instance of a broadly disseminated popular discourse about creativity, which, I will show, is thought of as a magical entity. The fact that the prize is creativity in the service of corporate capitalism for Gelb enhances the magic. There is also a vaguely fairytale-like character to the journey to genius Gelb offers. Why there should be such parallels is unclear: is it because there just *is* a set of patterns basic to the engaged human psyche,[2] or is it because motivational gurus see themselves as bringing enlightenment to the masses and therefore in need of speaking in what they imagine to be the language of the masses? Whichever, I would like to elaborate on some of the ways motivational speaking, personified in Gelb, overlaps with forms and topics that folklorists have found interesting.

Again, the basic form that defines motivational speaking is the sermon. The communication of information is subordinated to driving home, colorfully, a few memorable points, accompanied by the conjuring of inspiration and the hearer, it is hoped, being seized by energy and lifted out of daily torpor to a moment of vision, clarity, and renewed energy—much like that sought in traditional religious revival camps. Of the many specific methods the secular sermon borrows from the traditional sacred sermon, three stand out; they can be summarized as hagiography, magical thinking, and numerology.

HAGIOGRAPHY

First and most obvious, there is in Gelb a cult of saints, propelled by anecdotes and legends about larger-than-life heroes who epitomize what it is the audience aspires to. In the earlier book, Gelb offers Leonardo as a universal saint, while in *Discover Your Genius* he deals in a sort of hagiographic totemism in which the reader is invited to identify with one from a canonized list of creative individuals that includes Plato, Copernicus, Shakespeare, Gandhi, and Einstein, among others.

The title of both books contains the phrase "How to Think Like." The big question, of course, is, how *do* we learn to think like Leonardo or another of the top ten (actually, eleven with Leonardo)? The answer is that we learn largely by magic, a method that differs at least a little from what I think of as an academic approach (I elaborate on the nature of magical thinking below). I have been struck, for example, by the amount and complexity of the mathematics in the primary work of Copernicus, one of Gelb's geniuses. But we find almost no mathematics in Gelb's Copernicus, even though one of the best one-word answers to the question of how Copernicus thought is: mathematically.

Gelb's treatment of Plato is similar: from Plato's doctrine of the Forms, Gelb takes the message that Plato believed true wisdom and sense of beauty were to be discovered by looking inward. Plato's method, the classical dialectic, is barely mentioned, and only with the sentiment that it was a means by which a teacher helps a student discover true wisdom and beauty. There is no discussion of what the art of dialectic *really is* or of the most notorious use Plato made of it—a use that stands in direct opposition to Gelb's program—namely, to embarrass students by forcing them to confront their mentally slovenly, overly confident attitudes. Gelb does present and document, however, various general characteristics of his various geniuses' methods. He repeatedly mentions that they kept notebooks, engaged in a childlike free play of ideas and associations, and doodled and in general sought to visualize ideas and interconnections between them. He notes such things as part of an affirmative response to what he calls the "key question," namely: can the "fundamentals" or "essential elements" of "genius" be "abstracted" and made available to anyone?

Of course, all depends on what kind of, and how much, abstraction one is talking about: to go back to the earlier example, would Copernicus's mathematical skill have to be part of the abstraction? If, lacking the mathematical demonstrations, we developed a robust Copernicanism and went around boldly reversing paradigms, what we would have is the kind of buffoonish humor characteristic of some Native American clowning societies: facing the rear when riding a horse, rolling in dirt to wash oneself, climbing a ladder with your feet facing upward and your head down—such is a world of unmitigated, abstracted Copernicanism. We are forced to ask whether it was the boldness to think out of the box and reverse the usual paradigm that made Copernicus great (waiting until the end of his life to publish, was he that bold?); or might his greatness lie, rather, in his persistence in performing the minute and complex calculations necessary to prove that one among the many seemingly obvious paradigms in which we think is wrong. I submit that in the end Gelb is not trying to show us how to think like Copernicus but how to *get results* like Copernicus, precisely *without* having to learn to think like him. There is something vaguely American in his project. With supreme self-confidence as he solicits his audience's confidence in the product he peddles—confidence—Gelb's easy fervor calls to mind that great American archetype: the Confidence Man.

MAGICAL THINKING

As noted, Gelb does identify some general habits and strategies that might be useful to people who are stuck in a routine. But these habits and strategies imperceptibly blend into, indeed are overpowered by, something else. Gelb offers a number of cathartic or de-programming exercises based on sensation and tactility (and this correlates with Dolby's point about the call to de-socially condition ourselves), and early in the work he cautions that with your new perspective "you may . . . get a taste of the loneliness genius brings" (Gelb 1998:8).

Here is an example of a sensory-based de-programming exercise: "Buy three kinds of honey (e.g., orange blossom, wildflower, clover), open the jars, and smell each one for thirty seconds. Describe the aromas. Then taste each one in turn . . . Take a sip of springwater between tastes to clear your palate. Describe the differences in aroma and taste" (ibid.:129).

There are blindfolded-touching, wine-tasting, breathing, relaxation, and layered-listening exercises.[3] The imperative comes in part from the idea that intense sensation can shake one out of torpor and improve judgment and discrimination; but there also seems to be an assumption that the senses are less susceptible to social conditioning than are mind and, to some extent, emotions, so that sensation marks the level at which one begins to discover one's true self (at any rate, one will have something to do while at a business conference). Although perhaps superficially connected, what we have here is not the "take time to smell the flowers" of the 1960s, with the implication that this activity is an end in itself and an alternative to the corporate world, but rather smell the flowers in order to reboot your mind in order to succeed in capitalism.

The capitalist roots of Gelb's vision are quite transparent; citing Lisa Jardine's *Worldly Goods*, Gelb enthusiastically promotes the view that "the cultural and intellectual transformations of the Renaissance were driven by expanding capitalism" (ibid.:15), as if the intellectual transformations spawned by capitalism can be plowed back into it. It is not just we and Leonardo who are analogous, but, in Gelb's view, our epochs are as well. The epochal analogy underlies more specific analogies, such as that between you and Copernicus. Other exercises are based on contiguity or shared substance; it is as if you de-program yourself from your social-intellectual program to re-program yourself as an out-of-the-box thinker. An interesting irony: you are asked to get rid of your social programming because that is not the true you but are asked to re-program yourself with something, or rather someone, who is equally not you—unless, of course, you think Leonardo or Copernicus really is you, which is what you are encouraged to think throughout these works. The conflation is already evident in the double entendre title *Discover Your Genius*—your genius from the ten canonical geniuses and your genius within: they are the same person. This is a variation on a strategy of identification characteristic of cults of patron saints as well as much contemporary advertising, even though Gelb claims to be helping us escape the barrage of noise that reaches us from the latter, deadening our vitality and sapping our creativity.

For Gelb, creativity is the most ethereal of entities, yet it is approached through a kind of underlying materiality—and here we encounter a more interesting connection with magical thought, or at least ethnological theory of magical thought, from James Frazer to Claude Lévi-Strauss, which early on took inspiration from philosopher David Hume's principles of resemblance and contiguity. Gelb's seven da Vincian principles are named with Italian terms, and his book offers a number of Italian food recipes. Gelb's chapter on Copernicus recommends investing in a small telescope, and his treatment of Plato offers recommendations on giving a toga party complete with a recipe for "Symposium Lamb Delight" (Gelb 2002:49). Gelb relates Einstein's genius to his hair in much the same way Charles Reich, decades earlier in *The Greening of America* (1970), related the idea of liberation to the cut of bellbottom pants (and more could be explored in the parallels between these gurus of capitalism and anti-capitalism, respectively). Speak Italian, eat pasta, peer through the telescope, keep the notebook, wear the hair: you're on your way. It is also interesting to note how much of Gelb's chapter on Einstein is focused not on Einstein's theories but on the legends of Einstein's brain—the physical organ—which was actually preserved after Einstein's death and has been medically studied. Gelb reports: "One area of focus was the brain's 'glial' cells, which bind neurons (nerve cells) together and provide a medium for the transfer of electrochemical messages between them . . . [An] analysis of a slice of Einstein's brain demonstrated that it contained 400 percent more 'glial' cells per neuron than the average" (ibid.:319).

Gelb tells us that one acquires a lot of glial cells by having a stimulus-rich life, which from another angle supports the wine-tasting and other sensation exercises. So the logic of leading a stimulating life so you can think like Einstein, too, goes through a physical mediary: you have a stimulating life so your brain will develop as an imitation of Einstein's brain so you will be able to think like him and succeed in the world of corporate capitalism. Mythologist of modernity extraordinaire Roland Barthes (1995:69) summed up the legends that surround the medical preservation of Einstein's brain: "Paradoxically, the more the genius of the man was materialized under the guise of his brain, the more the product of his inventiveness came to acquire a magical dimension."

NUMEROLOGY

I have discussed hagiography and magical thought in Gelb's doctrine of creativity. Last, I turn to another characteristic motivational speaking shares with traditional mythological-folkloric forms and with self-help literature, namely, a predisposition to numerology, with a special interest in 3s and 7s—the mystical numbers of Western religious traditions. In Gelb these are interspersed with 10, the sum of 3 and 7. Ten, an even, nonprime number, tends to be for Gelb classificatory and hierarchical. As part of his sensory-tactility exercises he asks you to create lists of 10—10 important questions you should ask yourself, your top 10 classical and popular songs, and so on—and he is happy to offer suggestions. Ultimately, he asks you to pick your own from—or, rather, to pick yourself out of—the top 10 geniuses of all time. Three and 7, both prime numbers and also "odd" (as they say in mathematics), are more dynamic and processual. Seven is the number of basic da Vincian principles, beginning with *Curiosità*—each of which leads you into the next.

Patterns of 3 can also be seen in Gelb. One of his invocations of 3 can be traced to Sigmund Freud, who often thought in 3s, and beyond that to the same cultural unconscious that, I suspect, also gave us the 3-obstacles-overcome patterns of folk narrative as well as the high religious doctrine of the Trinity.[4] Freud gave us a history of the progress of science vis-à-vis our resistant anthropocentric inclinations, saying:

> In the course of centuries the *naive* self-love of men has had to submit to two major blows at the hands of science. The first was when they learnt that our earth was not the centre of the universe but only a tiny fragment of a cosmic system of scarcely imaginable vastness. This is associated in our minds with the name of Copernicus, though something similar had already been asserted by Alexandrian science. The second blow fell when biological research destroyed man's supposedly privileged place in creation and proved his descent from the animal kingdom and his ineradicable animal nature. This revaluation has been accomplished in our own days by Darwin, Wallace and their predecessors, though not without the most violent contemporary opposition. But human megalomania will have suffered its third and most wounding blow from the psychological research of the present time which seeks to prove to the ego that it is not even master in its own house, but must content itself with scanty information of what is going on unconsciously in its mind. (Freud 1964:284–85)

As I noted in *The Ancient Mythology of Modern Science* (Schrempp 2012a: chapter 6), this schema has been picked up by numerous popular science writers—including John Barrow (2005:220), Stephen Jay Gould (1997:17–19), and Daniel Dennett (1996:206)—and has given rise to an intriguing series of variants, which sometimes start to diverge significantly but, as if by a law of self-correction, keep coming back to a set of basic principles. Among the constants of the formula are the heroes themselves: the first two are invariably Copernicus and Darwin. Instead of a hero for the third slot, Freud names an emergent new academic field that will change everything, namely, psychoanalysis. As hero for this field, one can guess whom Freud had in mind. The same is true in virtually all later variants of this pattern in other writers. The final slot is often filled with an emergent contemporary field of scientific investigation, but one invariably close to the writer invoking the trinitarian formula. The variability of the third slot might seem to suggest a lack of pattern, yet within the variability lies a constancy: specifically, the third slot usually has something to do with the science of mind.

The schema I am describing here is also the schema of—and I would guess took its cue from—the idea of the Holy Trinity: the first person, the Father, is associated with creation, the design of the universe, who placed us in the center; the second person, the Son, is associated with the significance of our species. The third slot is once again characterized by highly variable iconography, most often that of wind or fire—things of marginal and evanescent materiality, common symbols of mystery stuff we label as mind or spirit. The Holy Spirit—or divine creative spirit—is the movement of divine energy in the here and now.

Freud's trinity presents a scientific alternative to this tri-level religiously anthropocentric vision. Freud's scheme moreover embodies the pattern of three obstacles overcome, each obstacle more difficult than the last: Copernicus undoes the cosmic design of God the Father (Copernicus was a cleric who shows no evidence of thinking that Freud's later verdict was what he was up to), Darwin undoes the work of the Son in giving us special significance. The third slot is invariably a scientific alternative to our claims of unique mind or spirit substance; computational theories of mind are among recent alternatives to the "science" of mind—psychoanalysis—Freud proffered for the third slot. In updating the Freudian trinity, it is as if popular science writers believe they are tracking the stirring of the spirit of science in our present moment, not to mention that they generate a lot of hot air and sometimes speak in tongues.

Within his robust numerology, it is clear that the science trinity has also found its way into Gelb's (2002) *Discover Your Genius*. Interestingly, in the earlier work, *How to Think Like Leonardo da Vinci*, Gelb (1998) also suggested 10 all-time geniuses, but the trinity was not yet among them. (Whom might he have read in the meantime?) At any rate, by the time of Gelb's 10 canonized geniuses, 3 are modern scientists: Copernicus, Darwin, and Einstein. Even the aspects of the third slot that seem to diverge from the pattern confirm it in a roundabout way; notably, the third slot remains the mind slot. Einstein's field was not mind or brain research; but, as noted, what Gelb talks about in his Einstein chapter is not Einstein's theories—which have to do with macrocosmic matters of time, space, matter, and energy—but rather Einstein's brain. It is a bit ambiguous whom we should take away as the real hero of the third slot: Einstein with the epitomizing brain or Gelb as another kind of brain-hero, the one who discovers the secret of how we can all have an Einstein brain for ourselves.

The number 3 for Gelb holds the same mesmerizing spell it does in Western folklore, myth, religion, and science; in the end, the journey to science is a journey we are all familiar with in the pattern of 3 obstacles overcome. How ideas and memorable formulas get passed around in popular literature is a topic with many potential analogies to folklore studies. The circulation is not just lateral but can be hierarchical in shifts of risen and sunken culture: Copernicus as hero of thinking is found not only in the maximally popularized writing of Michael Gelb but also in the abstruse metaphysics of Immanuel Kant (1965:21–22). Conceptually between Kant and Gelb lies an intriguing recent book by Howard Margolis (2002), *It Started with Copernicus,* a work with a sort of split personality. For in his detailed, scholarly treatment of Copernicus's thinking, Margolis shares the metaphysical gravitas of Kant; while in seeking to isolate, formularize, and make available for public-policy analysts the elusive Copernican magic—an acuity of thinking Margolis conveniently sums up as "Around the Corner Inquiry" ("AC Inquiry" for short)—Margolis ends up proffering a variation on Gelb-speak. Notable also is another book that appeared shortly after Gelb's (1998) book on Leonardo, Ben Shneiderman's (2003) *Leonardo's Laptop.* Despite the latter's more academically credentialed origins, Shneiderman's and Gelb's books are surprisingly parallel: whether through material culture (computers) or food-ways (pasta), they proclaim a vision of Leonardo as emblem of human creativity and ask how this elusive entity may be grasped. Almost certainly there will be another installment, perhaps with the title *How to Think Like Leonardo's Laptop* (or maybe like his smartphone).

NOTES

1. This chapter originated in a presentation given at the 2006 Hoosier Folklore Society's annual meeting in Terre Haute, Indiana, the theme of which was Fairytales and Creativity.

2. See Kurt Ranke's (1967) discussion of André Jolles's "Simple Forms."

3. Gelb has developed wine tasting as an avenue to improved creativity into a separate book, *Wine Drinking for Inspired Thinking* (Gelb 2010), with a preface "How to Drink Like Leonardo da Vinci."

4. Two classic folkloristic analyses of patterns of three are Axel Olrik(1965:133–34) and Alan Dundes (1968).

3

Opening the Two Totes
Mythos *and* Logos *in the Contemporary Agora-sphere*

DECEMBER 21, 2012: WINTER SOLSTICE AND TERMINUS of the Mayan calendar. Another day that will live in infamy? At this bottoming-out moment
of cosmic time I open Pandora's tote bag, which has rested inconspicuously
on a shelf in my study since 2004. The tote bag was part of the registration packet for an extravaganza conference (in Atlanta, GA, June 2–6,
2004) called "Mythic Journeys," sponsored by the Mythic Imagination
Institute, an organization of artists, scholars, and fans of mythology (in a
broad sense that includes, for example, fantasy literature and film). I came
to add the moniker "Pandora's" from a sense not of evil but of mischief and
from a conviction that many a mythic fall-from-paradise could equally be
imagined as a rise-from-monotony. The tote bag is black with a striking
white conference logo, accompanied by smaller-scale logos of the Joseph
Campbell Foundation, *Parabola Magazine*, Borders bookstore, and Krispy
Kreme doughnuts (more on this later). The cinch cord is arranged so the
tote can be worn as a backpack, as if anticipating the open road. To the
basic conference materials and schedule supplied with the tote I had added
a large sampling of informational brochures, advertisements, and other
"freebees" set out in standard conference fashion in the registration area,
before cinching up the cornucopia until an appropriate moment appeared
for its (re)opening.

On the same day, I also open a second bag, which has been sitting next
to Pandora's. This one is full of materials from another conference extravaganza that transpired two years earlier (in Burbank, CA, June 20–23, 2002),
the Fourth World Skeptics Conference sponsored by CSICOP (Committee
for the Scientific Investigation of Claims of the Paranormal), an organization of contemporary rationalists dedicated to loosening the grip of superstition and pseudo-science, from alien abductions to Ponzi schemes; CSICOP

DOI: 10.7330/9780874219708.c003

has since been renamed the Committee for Skeptical Inquiry (CSI).[1] One has only to thumb through CSICOP/CSI'S widely disseminated magazine, *Skeptical Inquirer*, to see that the term *myth* for them captures all that is defective in the conduct of human life. Both conference extravaganzas were set at important cyclic-calendric moments: Mythic Journeys was billed as a Joseph Campbell Centenary, while the Skeptics' conference came at the end of CSI's twenty-fifth anniversary year.

These two conferences, manifesting polar semantic valences of the term *myth*—our salvation vs. our downfall—have since fused in my mind as modern, popular manifestations of the venerable dichotomy of *mythos* and *logos* (loosely, divinely or poetically inspired story vs. rationally argued proposition), forever at the center of mythological inquiry.[2] This cognitive bonding of conferences was facilitated both by the semantic opposition and the similarity of venue. In each case we had a major conference, complete with "conference culture," by an organization that has some academic members and solicits academic input and backing but whose purpose is less the promotion of its views within academia than in the broader public arena. While both conferences were attended by people with a desire to improve themselves, the variety evident in both the offerings and the clientele gave rise in both cases to a spirit somewhat different than the type of conference alluded to in chapter 2— the one built around a program devised by one particular self-improvement specialist. In the time since the Mythic Imagination and CSI conferences, I have followed both organizations. I present here memories of these conferences filled out with themes that emerge in the two organizations (despite the considerable internal diversity within each), developed over a decade of myth watching in the popular sphere. Hereafter, these two organizations/conferences will be referred to, in shorthand, as the Mythics and the Skeptics.

Both the Mythics' and the Skeptics' conferences invited a significant folkloristic presence. The Skeptics featured a session on urban legends, in which Jan Brunvand gave an overview of his career-long research, while Tim Tangherlini gave an excellent presentation on the dynamics of urban-legend growth, including some generated by the 9/11 terrorist attack. The Snopes team also attended and discussed their popular website (Snopes.com) on urban legends and contemporary rumors. The Mythics invited academic mythologists from disciplines ranging from psychology to religious studies to folklore. Their conference had an archetypalist slant, emphasizing the legacies of Carl Jung and Joseph Campbell, but the conveners also invited mythologists with other theoretical leanings.

Although the urban-legends session at the Skeptics' conference was excellent, I was more intrigued by panels on topics to which I brought less familiarity, two in particular. At one of these a team of NASA scientists held a thought-provoking panel on the problem of scientists getting too person-ally attached to their theories and not knowing when to let go in the face of countervailing evidence. Their Power-Point presentations (then a new technique) were colorful and impressive, and the high drama with which they portrayed scientists retrenching in the face of crumbling paradigms amounted to a sort of performed version of Thomas Kuhn's (1962) clas-sic, *The Structure of Scientific Revolutions.* I encountered the NASA science team in matched blue blazers with NASA logo as they walked through the conference center; they reminded me of the Blue Angels sauntering out to their aircraft: competent, serious but jocular, professional, walking almost in formation.

The other memorable presentation was built around a magic show. Manifesting a long tradition, CSI employs magicians, as experts in decep-tion, to investigate faith healing and other practices they believe to be scams. At this conference one of the talks was by an academic psychologist who was also an amateur magician. His presentation incorporated a gimmick in which he exposed various strategies of prestidigitation while affecting other tricks—meta-magic, so to speak—he hoped his audience would not see through and that would leave them mystified and still bemused after his exercise in debunking. Which of his personalities won, rationalist or conjurer? His topic was the human predisposition to be trusting—a posi-tive characteristic, he averred, but one that can get us into trouble. But I do not recall the substance of his talk nearly as well as his earnestness—as an amateur magician striving and occasionally succeeding—in getting his tricks to work.

In the hallway of the Mythics' conference, one encountered not a sharply blazered team from NASA but satyrs and other fantasy-beings mixed in with "plain clothes" attendees. While some of the panels were fairly aca-demic, others were, or were constructed around, artistic performances. The main sessions were flanked by opportunities for participatory involvement in activities such as dream sharing, ecstatic dance, and yoga. The main pan-els were about exploring mythological themes in relation to literature, art, film, imagination, spirituality, personal growth, empowerment, and the moral uplift of contemporary society and culture. Those by academics were, expectedly, on the more analytical side. The inimitable Alan Dundes spoke on one of his usual topics, namely, genre differences, an intellectual concern for which he regarded folkloristics as carrying the banner: non-folklorists are prone to confusing and lumping together different oral narrative genres, especially myth and legend, while folklorists know that a myth is set in primordial time while a legend is set in historic time . . . and so on.[3] As is generally the case in popular usage, it was true that much of what fell under the rubric of "myth" at this conference would, in a more technically precise classification, fall under some other genre label such as folktale, legend, fantasy-literature, or science fiction. The tone of the conference was upbeat, but occasional presentations went in the other direction, addressing topics such as war. A well-known speaker on this topic was Sam Keen, who had co-produced the PBS documentary *Faces of the Enemy*. One of his conference presentation titles was "The Dark Side of Myth."

***

Both the Skeptics and the Mythics are earnest, and both think something is fundamentally awry in the way modern humanity engages the world and lives life. The word *free-thinkers* occurs in the self-description of each organization; and in the literature of each, one encounters advertisements for ocean cruises, dedicated to skepticism or, conversely, to the spirit and mystery of mythology. Greece is a destination for both sorts of cruise-pilgrimage. In the end, what is the difference?

The first and more obvious difference has to do with the role of science in human life and its relation to spirituality. It seems that neither group wholly rejects either science or spirituality and that the difference lies, rather, in the *relation between* the two. For the Mythics, spirituality seems to be temporally and logically prior to modern science and possibly threatened by it. By contrast, for the Skeptics, spirituality—if there is to be such, and many members seem to think there should be—is subject to vetting by science, with some sense that the highest, most right-minded sublimity should flow *from* science. Correlated with this difference is another: at least rhetorically, the Skeptics fear that too much is being admitted to the realm of the True, while the Mythics fear that too much is excluded from the True. The late Carl Sagan is a founding hero of CSI. As symptomatic of the Skeptics' mindset, consider the opening pages of chapter 13 ("Obsessed with Reality") of Sagan's (1996) *Demon-Haunted World*:[4] here you encounter a litany of ideas that many people do believe but *should not*, Sagan argues, because they are false. The list begins with astrology, the Bermuda Triangle, Big Foot and the Loch Ness monster, ghosts, the evil eye, halos around heads, and ESP—and goes on at a length that rivals medieval religious litanies (and no doubt has some overlap with them). For the Mythics, by contrast, consider a three-sentence passage on the back cover of the conference program:

> The Mythic Imagination Institute is a non-profit gang of infidels, orthodox free thinkers, Catholics, Jews, Pagans, Buddhists and others, who wish to

God that people would relax their grip on the Truth, with a capital T and get on with a wider view.

We are dying: we are all quite literally dying of smallness, exclusivity, moral certainty, self-righteousness, fundamentalism and bigotry. It's time to give everybody's story a chance. (Davis et al. 2004)

The middle sentence of this passage ("We are dying . . .") is problematic, for both Mythics and Skeptics regard themselves as offering the way out of smallness, fundamentalism, and bigotry. The way out espoused by the Skeptics emphasizes a rationalism that can include all members of the human community and that transcends the smallness, fundamentalism, and bigotry parochialism breeds; while the way out offered by the Mythics emphasizes an embracive pluralism—although a pluralism sometimes justified by its own kind of universalism, that of allegedly universal Jungian archetypes—so that any person's or culture's story is a version of the *one* story.

Scientific and Jungian forms of universalism would seem to diverge on their assessments of how well off humans are/were, spiritually and epistemologically, before the advent of modern science. The Mythics have greater trust in scientifically untutored immediacy in intuiting the world, placing faith in dreams, spontaneous emotion and imagination, and elementary strategies of intellectual synthesis and expression such as storytelling and song. The Skeptics, by contrast, regard the lot of primordial humanity as vulnerable and prone to superstition-inducing error and harmful fantasies that can only be dispatched through scientific investigation. For the Mythics, spirituality incorporates science, while for the Skeptics, science incorporates spirituality. The forms of spirituality espoused by both organizations could be termed *alternative*. The Skeptics' literature contains noticeable strands of agnosticism, atheism, and, correspondingly, secular spirituality. They challenge religious teachings that they regard as conflicting with science (one of the conference sessions was a debate with Christian fundamentalists on "intelligent design" creationism). The Mythics are more religiously inclined, although the major world religions sometimes take backstage to spiritual traditions seen as more primordially in tune with nature and as offering greater experiential immediacy and spontaneity. There is great interest in Native American spirituality and in revivals of archaic traditions such as neo-paganism.

A point of unexpected convergence between the two organizations lies in what one might conveniently term *guru dynamics*. There were examples of such dynamics at the Mythics' conference and one particularly striking instance in which a well-known panelist, who brought major guru status with him, became so entranced by his own charisma that he forgot there were other humans on his panel. One might expect the Skeptics, for their part, to shun guru dynamics or for that matter any "charismatic" process—any processes propelled by the personality rather than the proposition—as inherently irrational, but this is just not the case. I see little difference in the operation of, and audience susceptibility to, guru personalities in the two organizations and conferences.

The Skeptics, in fact, have many gurus, the most revered a range of celebrity scientists who write for *Skeptical Inquirer* and speak at CSI conferences (at this particular conference, artificial intelligence pioneer Marvin Minsky was a keynote speaker). CSI has actively promoted a sort of secular hagiography around Carl Sagan. The year 2013 was the fifth occurrence of Carl Sagan Day, celebrated on the hero's birthday, November 9. The Web announcement for CSI[5] lists a number of participating organizations, many campus- and student-based, throughout North America and other parts of the world.

The all but obligatory core of the Sagan Day celebration is a convivial screening of an episode of *Cosmos*, Sagan's groundbreaking television series.[6] The screening is typically accompanied by eating and drinking, discussions, speakers, readings from Sagan's works (one is tempted to say Scriptures), and tours of observatories and other science facilities. Some chapters of CSI have adopted apple pie as part of the ritual, either as featured food or as the price of admission. The apple pie is traced to the opening of one of the more famous episodes of *Cosmos*, "The Lives of the Stars," which begins with a dramatic close-up shot of pie dough being pressed, followed by Sagan saying, "If you wish to make an apple pie from scratch, you must first invent the universe." Perhaps this food choice—Skeptic's unleavened bread?—points to a day in which science is as American as apple pie. Another Sagan Day announcement from CSI, specifically its "grassroots" community and campus outreach segment, provides a range of links to various useful sources, including Sagan-related bibliography and other information sources, updates on the *Voyager* space probe (Sagan chaired the committee that chose the interstellar message *Voyager* carries), a site that shows how to dress like Sagan, other Sagan paraphernalia that includes earrings and coasters, and of course a CSI online store with coffee mugs and other standard CSI-monogrammed items.

Is the ritual accompanied by a myth? In a way it is: specifically, an embracive origin myth of science that Sagan recounts in a closing scene from "The Lives of the Stars," which I first encountered at a CSI celebration of Sagan's birthday held in an IMAX theater (the cake frosting for Sagan was blue; that for Darwin's birthday was brown, I assumed in homage to sky and primal ooze, respectively). Here Sagan invokes not the familiar narrative of science struggling upward out of primordial ignorance but rather science as converging with a mythic-archaic past. In a scene saturated with geological and cultural ancientness, Sagan, seated at the rim of the Grand Canyon, points to a pictorial representation, made by the Anasazi antecedents of the present-day Hopi people of the American Southwest, of what might be the eleventh-century explosion that produced the Crab Nebula. He also calls attention to the right-mindedness of traditional mythological views of the importance of the sun. In its fascination, awe, and commitment to observation, science emerges in Sagan's portrayal not in opposition to, but in common spirit with, ancient wisdom. This way of temporalizing science converges with the Mythics: both want an archaic, forever-defining experience of how humans should relate to the cosmos, which we can now recapture to energize our modern lives and recalibrate our course.[7]

If the operation of guru dynamics at the Skeptics' conference took me by surprise—as something I expected from Mythics but not Skeptics—then the equivalent, reciprocal surprise at the Mythics' conference was the greater visibility of "the marketplace." Or at least it seemed more visible; possibly I was merely taken by surprise, perhaps as a result of stereotypically associating stuff for sale in contemporary culture with a rationalistic "economic man" from which mythic man might seek escape. Both the Mythics and the Skeptics promote access to lectures, training sessions, information and publications, and decorative paraphernalia—for a fee. The difference may be more qualitative than quantitative; the Skeptics' offerings just seem spartan compared to the solicitations that pour forth from Pandora's tote bag: weekend retreats promising the discovery of my cosmic self, transformative massage therapy, shamanic studies, labyrinths, pilgrimages, initiations, Hildegard von Bingen and Loreena McKennitt CDs, art, dance, drumming, dramatic productions, tours of sacred landscapes.

Certainly, no large conclusion about the comparative relationship of money and ideas should be reached lacking a full investigation of the financial picture and philosophies of both conferences and organizations; I will say plainly that I do not see either organization or its leaders as more idealistically motivated than the other. Still, I do see an asymmetry, specifically, that the region of consciousness targeted by contemporary consumer advertising more readily adapts to the Mythics' mindset than to that of the Skeptics. But even without the research, one could guess that this would be the case. Just try to mentally entertain these advertisements: "Merry Christmas from *Skeptical Inquirer* magazine" or "Reason impels us to eat

Krispy Kreme doughnuts." The technological products of scientific rationality are an easy sell (cars, large flat-screen TVs, modern weapons systems), but scientific rationality itself, as an attitude or life principle, is a hard sell. Advertisers may try to tempt you with the scientific-technological sophistication of their product or may invoke rationality in appeals to the cost-conscious shopper; but such appeals are minor in comparison to, and are often co-opted into, the conjuring of desire.

Among the many talks and workshops listed in the program abstracts of the Mythics' conference is a talk titled "The Krispy Kreme Story" in which the company's CEO "discusses the visionary thinking and tactical plan that took Krispy Kreme from a $50 million company to a $2 billion company." Everybody's story should have a chance. For better or worse, rationally infused skepticism is at a disadvantage in immediacy of grab, as was recognized millennia ago by the Roman poet Lucretius who, adumbrating Sagan, sought to sweeten his plea for the rational life with honey from the Muses—specifically, his gifts as a mythologically inspired poet—as we will see in chapter 10.

It is the academic's livelihood to be critical. My criticisms of both organizations and conferences have to do with losing sight of the context. The Skeptics are prone to lose sight of how much—most obviously in the heroizing, narrativizing, ritualizing, and celebrating—they are adding to the revered principle of rationality. There is a looming gap between what is known (and perhaps even what *can be* known) through scientific rationality and what is necessary for human life, and it must be filled in with something. The Mythics—paradoxically, since they are "open"—are prone to lose sight of the lives of the "other," that is, the contexts of the different societies whose spiritual traditions they often want to emulate or incorporate. Losing sight of the other is facilitated by an archetypalist readiness to regard the mythic as universal and therefore as already belonging to everyone. Too easily they think the mythic can be extracted from one cultural form of life and incorporated into another. The aforementioned pluralism of the Mythics bespeaks a popular variety of cultural relativism that has lost sight of the fact that cultural relativism originally carried the conviction not just that many human ways of life are viable but that particular customs are *relative to*—that is, take their meaning from—the particular cultural contexts in which they occur.

Nearly all of the conferences I attend are "academic conferences"; these two were exceptions. I have significant disagreements with both organizations, but also, in both cases, I find it intriguing and energizing to discover a broader public interest in issues I deal with daily as "academic." If a bit less dramatically than the ancient Greek philosopher Diogenes the Cynic, who lived in a storage jar to put into the public gaze his philosophy of simplicity and contempt for pretense, the major impetus of both organizations is toward promoting, in the public arena, a message about life well-lived. In the face of the insularity of American academic life, such organizations, along with our students actually going out into the world, can serve as a reminder to academics that ideas are never "merely academic."

NOTES

1. Full disclosure: the CSI "bag" is imaginary—or, if you prefer, a "literary device"—since, unlike "Mythic Journeys," the Skeptics' conference did not provide an actual bag (is this significant?); what I have for the latter is conference materials, notes, and memories. See comparative mythologist James Frazer's (1984) classic article on the mythic theme of the two trees: the Tree of Life and the Tree of Death. I leave it to the reader to decide which tote is which.

2. For two of the more stimulating discussions of the perennial dichotomy, see Vernant (1984); Lincoln (2000).

3. Dundes essentially followed the oral narrative genre distinctions set out by William Bascom, in a classic article Dundes included in his myth-theory anthology *Sacred Narrative* (see Bascom 1984).

4. This book, especially chapters 10 ("The Dragon in My Garage") and 12 ("The Fine Art of Baloney Detection"), is all but canonical for many CSI members. In chapter 17 ("The Marriage of Skepticism and Wonder"), Sagan discusses CSICOP, defending it against the charge that it is a new Inquisition opposed to human wonder.

5. At http://www.centerforinquiry.net/carlsaganday.

6. *Cosmos* (2000) was not the first instance of television promotion of science (see chapter 6, on the science programs produced by Frank Capra), but it moved such popularizing into a new era of glitz, made possible in part by computer-generated "effects."

7. This sort of mythologizing move is recurrent in Sagan. Consider once again *The Demon-Haunted World*, which was published just before the end of the twentieth century. Sagan, in a move that in other contexts he would certainly criticize as irrational, takes advantage of the fear of degeneration that invariably intensifies as civilizations approach the end of their major calendar cycles. He expresses concern that in the near future science will be buried by pseudo-science: "The candle flame gutters. Its little pool of light trembles. Darkness gathers. The demons begin to stir" (Sagan 1996:27). Sagan proclaims, "A proclivity for science is embedded deeply within us, in all times, places and cultures" (ibid.:317). His fear is not that science won't begin but that, having begun everywhere, we moderns may lose it and thus, in effect, betray our primordial birthright. As if in support, he cites ethnographic research on the !Kung San, Kalahari hunter-gatherers, seemingly chosen to represent a rudimentary stage of human technological development. Summarizing their method for tracking the footprints of their prey, Sagan comments that it "is essentially identical to what planetary astronomers use in analyzing craters" (ibid.:313). Another instance is found in the opening lines of Sagan's *Pale Blue Dot*, which urges the resumption of space exploration after the fallow period that followed the Apollo moon missions. His opening line is, "We were wanderers from the beginning" (Sagan 1994:xi); he goes on to portray space exploration as

the contemporary manifestation of the nomadic spirit of archaic hunter-gatherers. Further commentary on mythologizing in "The Lives of the Stars" and in Sagan's work more generally can be found in Schrempp (2012a, chapter 6; 2012b).

4

Taking the Dawkins Challenge
On Fairy Tales, Viruses, and the Dark Side of the Meme

THE PREVIOUS TWO CHAPTERS DEALT WITH INDIVIDUALS' dissatisfaction with themselves or the prevailing worldview of their societies and with attempts, many alluding to or inspired by "folk" remedies, to diagnose and correct the perceived defects. This chapter deals with the now broadly familiar concept of the "meme" and how this concept, too, in surprising ways, has been drawn into discourses about personal and societal pathologies and their remedies. I briefly discuss three levels at which memes are drawn into moral discourse, each of which I find highly problematic. One level is nothing less than "the problem of evil"—that is, the ultimate philosophical question of why there is evil in the world—a question some theorists think the concept of the meme can answer. But when the meme is posed as the answer to the problem of evil, meme theory, I argue, starts to resemble folk-religious theology.

The first level at which the concept of the meme has entered moral discourse lies in the overall characterization of the role of the meme in the evolution of culture. Importantly, the idea of the meme was originally announced in a notably upbeat moral tone. One of the most frequently quoted passages concerning memes stems from Richard Dawkins's original formulation in *The Selfish Gene*:

> Examples of memes are tunes, ideas, catch-phrases, clothes fashions, ways of making pots or of building arches. Just as genes propagate themselves in the gene pool by leaping from body to body via sperms or eggs, so memes propagate themselves in the meme pool by leaping from brain to brain via a process which, in the broad sense, can be called imitation. If a scientist hears, or reads about, a good idea, he passes it on to his colleagues and students. He mentions it in his articles and his lectures. If the idea catches on, it can be said to propagate itself, spreading from brain to brain. (Dawkins 1989:192)

DOI: 10.7330/9780874219708.c004

Note that all of these examples are things humans value: pots, bridges, tunes, fashions, and good scientific ideas. Propagation is analogized to a process most humans value positively: sexual reproduction. In a recent article, Jack Zipes (2008) takes meme theory into the realm of social custom, arguing that the fairy tale "The Frog King" as a discourse on mating strategies has disseminated memetically. In accord with the positive tone of the passage by Dawkins quoted above, Zipes notes that "memetic force . . . cannot drive the spread of the tale unless it benefits humans and their need to adapt to their environment" (ibid.:114). Since theoretical characterizations of memes are prone to anthropomorphizing anyway, there is no reason not to conclude from such comments by Dawkins and Zipes that memes are our friends. This culture-building property of the meme has attracted some folklorists and anthropologists to the concept and has also given rise to the criticism that this has all been done before under the rubrics of "trait," "motif," "tale-type," and "cultural configuration"—the analytical concepts used in the pre-meme era to trace the process and routes of geographic dissemination of culture or traditional stories.

But right from the start, this culture-building function of the meme was accompanied by morally negative insinuations. Foremost is the "selfish" theme from the "selfish gene" root metaphor, but one also encounters a series of analogies to entities and processes humans regard negatively: disease, viruses, and epidemiology. Anthropomorphized in these terms, it seems in the very nature of memes, even good ones, to behave badly. Memes are like politicians: even those whose intentions are ultimately altruistic will not remain what they are unless they win; hence, they are necessarily pushy, exploitive, and self-promoting in the pursuit of their beneficent goals.[1] The morally ambivalent quality of memes also recalls many of the characters one encounters in traditional mythologies, another realm in which humans externalize their views and anthropomorphize the world around them. In the Greek poet Hesiod's *Theogony*, for example, Zeus ultimately emerges as the shaper of the just political realm, but he does so only through a range of deceitful and self-promoting acts that put him in a position to be the dispenser of fairness. Plato's take on Hesiod's vulgarization of the doings of the gods is a founding text for the skepticism toward mythology in the Western intellectual tradition. In his *Republic*, Plato says:

> Then our program of education must begin with censorship. The censors will approve the fables and stories they deem good and ban those they consider to be harmful . . .

> First of all, I mean the greatest and most malevolent lies about matters
> of the greatest concern: what Hesiod said Uranus did to his son Cronos
> and how Cronos revenged himself on his father. Then there is the tale of
> Cronos's further doings and how he suffered in his turn at the hands of
> his own son, Zeus. Even were these stories true, they ought not to be told
> indiscriminately to young and thoughtless persons. It would be best if they
> could be buried in silence. If they absolutely must be retold, it should be
> only to a chosen few under conditions of total secrecy. And this only after
> performing a sacrifice not of an ordinary pig but of some huge and usually
> unprocurable victim. That should help cut down the number of listeners.
> (Plato 1985:73–74 [377–78])

As dictated by their very nature, a certain amount of sleaze necessarily runs through the life of all memes. As Plato suggests in regard to mythology, perhaps that is part of the attraction; like myths, memes are us.

But there is a second dimension of darkness in memes. At issue here is not memes (and this means all memes) behaving badly but, rather, *intrinsically* bad memes, specifically memes whose very content depicts and promotes evil moral attitudes and actions among humans: the meme that we should eat our children, for example. Here meme theory confronts the "problem of evil," by which I mean the longstanding insight, reflected in traditional religious and ethical thought, that life contains morally negative qualities, regarding which we cannot but ask, why? When meme theory confronts the problem of evil, it can take some interesting turns, which I will illustrate through two recent works: Richard Dawkins's (2006) *The God Delusion,* and Jack Zipes's (2006) *Why Fairy Tales Stick,* in which Zipes further elaborates on his views, mentioned earlier, regarding memes and fairy tales. These two books, one by a biologist, the other by a literary scholar, are both largely about evil memes and are parallel in many other ways.[2]

The first thing that happens when meme theory confronts the problem of evil is that memes suddenly seem to lose their capacity for doing any good at all. The further we proceed—into the woods, so to speak—in Zipes's and Dawkins's books, the less evil vs. good is cast as bad meme vs. good meme and the more it is cast as memes vs. some meme-transcending power that we, or at least some of us, possess. Evil memes are not something that good memes must overcome but rather something that we humans must overcome. The evil memes that most concern Zipes are those belonging to fairy tales (or should we say that the fairy tales belong to the memes?), while those that concern Dawkins belong to religions more broadly. For both authors, moral darkness is epitomized in the abuse of children—for Zipes, in the fairy tales of eating children and in other traditional literatures, such as the biblical story of Abraham sacrificing his son Isaac (see especially Zipes 2006, chapter 7). The lack of reference to good memes stepping in to put a stop to all this suggests that memes are not enough to correct for such moral darkness.

But if good memes do not correct for bad memes, whence comes the power of doing so? For both Dawkins and Zipes, the antidote to evil memes seems to reside in some meme-transcending power of critical thought. For Dawkins, this is a kind of scientific rationalism that is almost necessarily atheistic, since in his view religion is a reservoir of evil memes. For Zipes, the antidote seems more of an enlightened, critical humanism buttressed by social science.

But there is a serious methodological problem here—specifically, that if one is to identify memes on the basis of persistence and recurrence, one could put the confrontation between good and evil fully on a memetic basis. All the way back to the pre-socratic philosophers, one could, if so inclined, reconstruct a memetic prehistory for the ideas Dawkins and Zipes put forward as enlightened correctives to prevailing evil memes. One could find among Greek philosophers many varieties of religious skepticism memes, humanism memes, social reform memes, pedagogy memes, and so on. So the question is: why, within the heart of darkness, do Dawkins and Zipes ultimately resist portraying the battle against evil as a historical jostling of evil and good memes? Why, in other words, do they curtail the theory to which they have committed their main efforts?

It is possible to be very specific here. Zipes (ibid.:224) actually cites episodes from Greek mythology as evidence of the ancientness of the bad meme of eating our children; that is what Cronus does, swallows his children. But these actions are also the precise object of Plato's criticisms in the passage quoted earlier, in which he recoils from such accounts, claiming that such actions must be dismissed as un-godlike and thus not be passed on indiscriminately.

Zipes says, "No matter what position we take with regard to tradition, it is clear that the past can devour us, as we devour our children, if our position is not critical and transformative" (ibid.:241). Anyone can disagree with Plato's specific correctives, but critical and transformative is precisely what he was attempting to be in confronting traditions of gods eating their kids. So, why not present Plato as an early host for the anti-child-ingestion meme, which, out of self-interest, gained a foothold in what was to be one of the world's most canonically reproduced texts, or meme hosts, *The Republic*; whence it leaped (perhaps through intermediaries) to Zipes as a new, contemporary host of this selfish meme. This good (albeit selfish) meme could also be listed alongside the pots, arch bridges, tunes, and other good things memes now bring us (which mythic culture heroes used to bring us).[3] The battle of good and evil would be symmetrical: a battle of meme vs. meme.

One possible source of resistance to the image of evil and good memes battling it out is that no culture critic would like to emerge as a mere meme minion—that is, as a device used by memes, even if they are good memes, for propagating themselves. The source of such resistance may be quite lofty: the very notion of goodness without a willful subject, or without room for moral heroism in the face of external threat, offends our idea of what moral goodness is. But there are also parochial, anthropocentric, and potentially hegemonic dimensions. We also like to think of the possibility of such moral heroism as part of our vocation as humanistic scholars. Indeed, the vision of religion and folktales as carriers of bad memes, ones our critical thinking can combat, affirms that our role as humanistic scholars is necessary if the world is to be good. Preserving tradition "while standing outside it and transforming it" is a power Zipes (ibid.:242) accords to great storytellers, but the great storytellers he names are figures from the intellectual class (notably Ernst Bloch, Bertolt Brecht, and Walter Benjamin), of which Zipes and many readers of this chapter are members.

The vision has resonance with the Enlightenment view of a priesthood of thinkers stemming the tides of the unthinking darkness of the masses as perpetrated through religion and oral tradition. Maybe this vision should be considered as an academic meme that took off during the Enlightenment (although it, too, can be traced at least back to Plato). Religious traditions sometimes see good as well as evil as emanating from outside forces operating through us ("God's saving grace"),[4] but academics feel more proprietary toward the good they see themselves as doing. Zipes guardedly admits to the idea that some storytelling traditions are counter-canonical. However, for him the bigger source for counter-canonical views seems to lie outside of traditional storytelling communities and in the realm of cosmopolitan intellectuals and scientists, a realm that appears to be meme-free (or at least we hear nothing from Zipes about the operation of memes within this realm).

But I see yet another possibility—namely, that meme theory, confronting the problem of evil, is drawn toward, if not into, traditional religious paradigms for dealing with the problem of evil. Judaeo-Christian moralizing, for example, shows a tendency to align the material and the biological with the imperfect or evil, as if matter is inherently morally compromised. The antidote must be found in some realm that transcends matter, its limitations, and its mechanics. Memes are not material things, and yet they are defined through robust biological analogy and materialistic mechanics.

Dawkins has been criticized repeatedly for biological reductionism. But I find his most interesting characteristic to lie in the opposite direction— namely, that despite the biologizing, he appears to hold out for a realm of moral reflection that transcends not only genes but memes, a realm he does not adequately elaborate in relation to either. Dawkins concludes his announcement of the concept of the meme: "We are built as gene machines and cultured as meme machines, but we have the power to turn against our creators. We, alone on earth, can rebel against the tyranny of the self-ish replicators" (Dawkins 1989:201). This comment and others suggest a phenomenology of moral reason that has no clear relation to the scheme of influence and causation he sets up in his concept of the meme or to the processes of Darwinian evolution to which he is committed. One of the religious conceits to which meme theory has been drawn, in other words, is the anthropocentric conviction that we humans enjoy a unique spontaneity of moral will within an otherwise deterministic cosmos—a rather standard point of religious resistance to the advance of science. In the 1989 edition of *The Selfish Gene*, Dawkins answers the charge that he is ultimately a dualist who allows free will into his seemingly deterministic biological evolutionism by appealing to the difference between statistical determinacy and the deter-minacy of any particular instance (ibid.:331–32). But Dawkins's response is entirely inadequate to the charge; it is a sort of "Lucretian swerve" for his twenty-first-century biology.[5]

One can find numerous other similarities between evil memes and tra-ditional religious ways of conceptualizing evil. For example, in both meme theory and traditional religious demonology, the power of evil is dramatized by positing an external agency with its own volition and will to invade and take possession of us. At one point Zipes deploys meme rhetoric, along with his dominant trope—the devouring of children—to characterize tradition: "tradition feeds off the young to maintain itself and will do anything to pre-serve itself, including the sacrifice of the young" (Zipes 2006:235–36).[6] For whatever psychological reasons, we seem to find such attribution of external agency a compelling dramatization of the presence and problem of evil in our world.

In the Gospel of Mark (Mark 5:8–16), Jesus confronts a man with an unclean spirit:

> He said unto him, Come out of the man, thou unclean spirit. And he asked him, What is thy name? And he answered, saying, My name is Legion: for we are many. And he besought him much that he would not send them away out of the country. Now there was there . . . a great herd

of swine feeding. And all the devils besought him, saying, Send us into the swine, that we may enter into them. And forthwith Jesus gave them leave. And the unclean spirits went out, and entered into the swine: and the herd ran violently down a steep place into the sea . . . and were choked in the sea.

In the secular, Darwinian world, Legion's new name is Memeplex. As defined by Dawkins, memeplexes are groups of mutually sustaining memes that travel and invade in packs. One of the pernicious religious memeplexes Dawkins presents is the bundle which includes the ideas that one survives one's death, that martyrs go to paradise, that heretics should be killed, and that faith (or belief without evidence) is a virtue (Dawkins 2006:199).

So, what do we have when modern meme theory meets the old philosophical "problem of evil"? One possible answer is that we have a new mythology, one that, like all mythologies, plays on a particular society's ontology, its concept of ultimate reality—whether that concept is built around invasive demons or genes—to account for and dramatize the problem of evil. The other possible answer is that what we have here is finally science: memes as the demythologized, empirically and rationally verified entities that lie behind our archaic religious illusions. My own sympathies are with the former view,[7] although if I am wrong on this but right that memes in the context of the problem of evil are drawn toward preexisting religious paradigms (or memeplexes, if you will), the situation is even more interesting: it would illustrate the power of religious forms over even their detractors.

A third dimension of memes and morality concerns the worldview promoted by Dawkins's science. This is the most complex dimension, but I can give only a sketch. Briefly, well after *The Selfish Gene*, Dawkins (1998) published a book titled *Unweaving the Rainbow* to counter the coldness perceived in his earlier book. In *Unweaving*, Dawkins attempts to distinguish bad from good poetic science; we can be scientists and poetic as long as we engage in good poetic science. As an example of bad poetic science, Dawkins cites a book jacket blurb that reads "A masterly description of the evolving, musical, nurturing and essentially caring universe." Dawkins explains: "Even if 'caring' were not a limp cliché, universes aren't the sort of entities to which a word like caring can sensibly be applied" (ibid.:188–89). But then in parentheses he adds: "I realize that I am vulnerable to the criticism that a gene is not the sort of entity to which a word like 'selfish' should be applied. But I vigorously challenge anyone to maintain the criticism after reading *The Selfish Gene* itself, as opposed to just the title" (ibid.:189). Dawkins thus asserts that his own anthropomorphic title is redeemed by the book that bears it. But he does not name the book that bears the bad poetic blurb; so for years after *Unweaving* was published, readers had no easy way to check whether the offending blurb might not similarly be redeemed by the book to which it is attached. My colleague Bill Hansen, using recent search technology, discovered that the blurb, attributed to John F. Haught, appears on the jacket of Louise Young's (1993) *The Unfinished Universe*. Upon perusal, I find as much to be skeptical about in Young's portrayal of the evolving universe as in Dawkins's portrayal of memes; but I do not find "caring" to be more misleading than "selfish."

That is the Dawkins challenge: to read *The Selfish Gene* and still dare to be critical of his anthropomorphizing title. I accept the challenge because, having read the book several times, I see no basis for ruling out warm anthropomorphizing of the cosmos while allowing cold anthropomorphizing. One trope is as valid as the other for the purpose of scientific metaphor, since some aspects of our cosmic ambient sustain us while others harm us. The asymmetry in Dawkins betokens some larger ideology and perhaps also a difference between half-empty vs. half-full cosmic temperaments. For Dawkins, the admission of anything other than coldness and selfishness into the fundamental matter of the cosmos would seem to run contrary to the necessary worldview of science and to the moral heroism of the scientist. Indeed, the coldness of the cosmos provides the dramatic backdrop for such heroism.

The moral ramification of the concept of the meme is tricky business. Much of meme theory, specifically the part that deals with cultural dissemination, *has been done before*—less ideologically and more scientifically, I suggest—under the labels of "trait" and "motif." The idea of the meme is new and challenging precisely because complex moral connotations, even a moral worldview, are loaded onto it. But I suggest that the moral connotations now loaded into the meme *have also been done before* in the form of folk-religious ideas about the origin and nature of evil. As in all science and even more so in science popularization and promotion, it behooves us to stay alert so we may not be snatched by morally repugnant memes (or viruses or malevolent motifs or bad ideas even) and so we may not be unnecessarily bedeviled by something new that is old.

NOTES

1. "All tales want to stay alive in us, and they compete for our attention. However, only certain ones remain with us, catch on, attach themselves to our brains so that we will remember them and propagate them" (Zipes 2006:27). Such is the typical rhetoric of the meme

found throughout Zipes and Dawkins. Even though Zipes periodically insists that humans sometimes exert an agency or control over the circulation of memes, the rhetoric of the meme remains dominantly one of memes self-interestedly exerting their influence over us. For a philosophical discussion of the problem of agential language in memes and evolutionary theory more generally, see Godfrey-Smith (2010: chapter 8).

2. Some of the tendencies I discuss can also be seen in Dennett (2006); Brodie (2009); and Ray (2009).

3. Zipes cites the passage about pots, bridges, and so on I quoted above at the opening of his book (Zipes 2006:4). Ironically, he quotes it again near the end (ibid.:230), seemingly not noticing how out of place the good memes mentioned in the passage are in his own closing arguments.

4. A particularly intriguing recent invocation of external forces operating morally through us—intriguing just because it is made by another major popular science writer who, like Dawkins, veers away from spiritual explanations—is the iconic phrase from Abraham Lincoln in a recent title, Steven Pinker's (2011) *The Better Angels of Our Nature: Why Violence Has Declined.* "Better angels" would seem to belong to the same realm of morally laden, anthropomorphic metaphor as "selfish gene."

5. First-century BCE Roman atomist Lucretius posited that, in falling, certain atoms swerve, thus introducing indeterminacy into the cosmos. The Lucretian swerve has come to be seen as a sort of archetype (arche-meme?) of smuggling free will into scientifically explanatory schema that otherwise militate against them (cf. Horgan 1997:17). To be sure, Dawkins does give considerable attention to the origin and development of the morally good under the rubric of altruism. The first and most obvious evolutionary explanation for altruism lies in the benefit for certain gene pools of individual self-sacrifice, even though this will not benefit the particular sacrificing organism. Beyond this, Dawkins also accounts for altruism as a side effect of some other trait selected for or a selection that occurred in a context that has since changed. For example, our urge to altruism, generosity, empathy, and pity evolved in a context in which "we had the opportunity to be altruistic only towards close kin and potential reciprocators. Nowadays that restriction is no longer there, but the rule of thumb persists" (Dawkins 2006:221). Dawkins refers to such non-utilitarian altruism as Darwinian "misfirings" or "mistakes: blessed, precious mistakes" (ibid.). As far as it goes, Dawkins's evolutionistic account of the origins of altruism is not implausible. What remains unaccounted for is the evolution and nature of the perspective from which Dawkins (or anyone) judges certain evolutionary consequences (such as the triumph of specific memes) to be a morally negative development while judging other evolutionary developments to be morally "precious." Dawkins (1993, for example) unconvincingly attempts to distinguish memes from mental viruses. In a thoughtful critique, Kate Distin points out that Dawkins's attempt rests not on a difference of mechanism but on a differential valuation of meme contents: "Dawkins comes perilously close to labelling only those things of which he approves, as 'great' and nonviral" (Distin 2005:74). Distin's critique, as I read it, confirms through another route what I argued earlier, that for Dawkins a level of moral consciousness exists and operates beyond the realm of memes, judging which of them are good and bad. Thanks to Elliott Oring for bringing Distin's commentary to my attention. See also Dawkins's discussion of the attractions of dualism (Dawkins 2006:179–81).

6. Zipes repeats the sentiment again a few pages later, with respect to the past, in the passage quoted earlier about the past devouring us as we devour our children.

7. The anthropomorphizing that goes on in the name of memes is one indication that we are in the realm of myth. Such anthropomorphizing is elaborated with relish and thus

should not be confused with the inescapable anthropomorphizing scientists acknowledge as the given condition of human language. To anthropomorphize, for science, is to make less real; while for myth, it is to make more real.

5

The Biggest Losers
A Sensible Plan for Controlling Your Cosmic Appetite

IN HIS MODERN CLASSIC *MYTHOLOGIES*, ROLAND BARTHES (1995) applies the term *myth* to cultural-political ideologies embodied in everyday French and American middle-class popular entertainments, food preferences, social attitudes, and material paraphernalia—such as toys, laundry detergent, and magazines. Barthes's usage is jolting and problematic for scholars who wish to reserve "myth" for grand cosmological narratives. However, the discord lessens, or at least takes a new turn, as one realizes that Barthes's vignettes on everyday life typically implicate grand and often archaic dimensions. For example, in "The Face of Garbo," Barthes alludes to themes of the eternal or archetypal in human countenance; in "Soap-Powders and Detergents," the ancient four-element theory of earth, air, water, and fire; in "The Jet-Man," the major epochs of Christendom; and in "The Brain of Einstein," the human predilection for localizing magical powers in material objects (as in the case of Gelb's Einstein, considered in chapter 2). Barthes could be read as a new use of the term *myth* or, alternatively, as a recognition of the traditionally mythic in modern, everyday guise.

The following vignette is inspired by Barthes's method of connecting the modern quotidian with the grandly cosmic—except that while Barthes begins with everyday ideologies and then alludes to their cosmic resonances, I move in the opposite direction, beginning with two recent books about scientific cosmology and then, through a modern parable, suggesting the interrelation between them and contemporary everyday food ideologies.

The sympathy between realms to which I call attention might be seen as a new variation on an old mythic conceit, for many traditional mythologies and their associated rituals are built around the conviction that the cosmic and the quotidian express the same patterns at different scales: the shape of the cosmos mirrors the shape of the village; the errors that transpired at

DOI: 10.7330/9780874219708.c005

the moment of creation continue to crop up as the defects of everyday life; the ritual that promotes local well-being does so by promoting the cosmos's favorable disposition toward human existence in general. We will encounter another variation on this conceit in the book's concluding chapter, since the roman poet Lucretius also seeks to alleviate human anxieties through a diagnostic method that correlates the personal with the cosmic.

***

The cosmic picture to be considered in the present chapter is put forward in two books by the husband and wife team Joel Primack and Nancy Ellen Abrams—who are, respectively, a professor of physics at the University of California Santa Cruz and an attorney working in public policy. Their main work is *The View from the Center of the Universe* (Primack and Abrams 2006). In 2009 they were invited to give the prestigious Terry Lectures at Yale University; from these came a second, short book (this time by Abrams and Primack), *The New Universe and the Human Future* (Abrams and Primack 2011). I greatly condense long, detailed discussions into basic claims that define Primack and Abrams's project.

The most important claim infusing Primack and Abrams's work is that it is a morally good thing for humans to connect emotionally with the cosmos—that is, to regard the cosmos as a *home* rather than as random, alien matter—but that it is difficult for people born into a scientific worldview to connect to the cosmos in such an effusive way. Primack and Abrams cite two impediments, summarized in the names Copernicus and Thomas Kuhn. The former has become the emblem of human cosmic dethroning, while the latter, in his influential book *The Structure of Scientific Revolutions* (Kuhn 1962), is associated with the conviction—which Primack and Abrams think has also infused public consciousness—that science is incapable of giving us a stable vision of the cosmos since it keeps overturning its teachings.

For Primack and Abrams, emotionally connecting with the cosmos means seeing ourselves as occupying the center of the universe—in other words, adopting an anthropocentric stance. They do not really explore the possibility of non-anthropocentric ways of emotionally connecting with the cosmos, of which there are some well-known attempts. The most oft-quoted are from Nobel Prize–winning physicist Steven Weinberg, who is known for his insistence that science requires emotional austerity and existential courage; yet even Weinberg conveys an image of the cosmos as a cozy parlor in a winter snowstorm, leaving cosmic solace-seekers with at least some consolation. In an interview Weinberg commented, "Although we are not the stars in a cosmic drama, if the only drama that we're starring in is one that we're making up as we go along, it's not entirely ignoble that faced with this unloving, impersonal universe we make a little island of warmth and love, and science and art, for ourselves. That's not entirely despicable."[1]

Weinberg is claiming that humans can find meaning in the cosmos without being anthropocentric; intriguingly, his view resonates with a very old notion of "cosmos." For in at least some of the usages in Greek mythology, such as the one we find in Hesiod's *Theogony*, *cosmos* seems to imply something like an island of order surrounded by Chaos.

There is a rhetorical divide faced by those who want cosmic solace in the post-Copernican universe: to go with the Weinberg kind (we are *not* the center, but we can create for ourselves a heroic sense of meaning anyway) or to go with a new version of the pre-Copernican kind (we *are* the center, in some hitherto unrecognized sense). Primack and Abrams offer the latter, developed through a two-pronged approach. Both prongs raise intriguing issues in regard to traditional mythology and its alleged perennial defect, anthropocentrism. The first prong consists of the conviction that modern cosmology reveals new ways in which we are *objectively* at the center of the cosmos, even though we are not at the *spatial* center, as many traditional origin myths would have it. Luckily for us, "We finally have the opportunity to end this alienation" (Primack and Abrams 2006:4), for modern science can uncover ways to gratify—without illusion—our emotional need to be at the center of the cosmos. For example, according to Primack and Abrams, we occupy a central position in *cosmic time*, specifically, the moment in which the universe has expanded enough to allow life and consciousness to evolve but not so far that its components are out of range of one another: we thus occupy the one "central" moment in which the universe can be known from the inside. Now, this point is interesting; but, a mythologist might object, it is not the same thing as Zeus trying to hold the cosmos together through various scheming consorts and squabbling children. Traditional mythologies are filled with the drama of humanlike personalities engaged in humanly familiar situations, all of this magnified by larger-than-life gods. Does the new scientific anthropocentrism really speak to the same realm of fascination and desire as the old?

The second prong might seem more promising in terms of filling the void left by scientifically now-discredited mythologies. For although Primack and Abrams insist that scientific claims must supersede those of traditional origin myths, they also claim that some traditional mythico-religious visions of the cosmos can be usefully salvaged and re-purposed. This is in part because the findings of modern cosmological science are often so counterintuitive that they can be grasped only through complex metaphors, and religious mythology is a source of such metaphors. Hence, for example, the mystical teachings of Kabbalah offer images useful in conceptualizing states of energy in the cosmos, while Polynesian cosmic genealogies resonate with scientific attempts to understand the first moments of the cosmos. Egyptian preoccupation with the connection between the present day and the deep cosmic past finds resonance with the attitude of contemporary scientific astronomy. Some of Primack and Abrams's choices leave one wondering; for example, they select the mysterious pyramid and eyeball that appears on every US dollar bill as an emblem of the hierarchical organization of matter in the cosmos, broad at the base and narrowing to a tip that reflects the rarity of life in the universe. Not since Max Weber's placement of *Poor Richard's Almanac* at the center of his classic *The Protestant Ethic and the Spirit of Capitalism* has a scholarly analysis so surprisingly interconnected US money and cosmology.

Such attempts to salvage and re-purpose traditional mythologies may on the surface appear closer to filling the void left by the old ones, but this is accomplished only at the cost of significant dilution. First, the re-purposed mythologies, compared with the originals, will be partial, for the scientific vetting process will have to eliminate some aspects: "Many religions have concepts that resonate harmoniously with aspects of the new scientific picture—concepts that can, in fact, help us tremendously to appreciate the depth and meaning of the universe—but all religions also have concepts that don't. An attempt to explain the modern universe in terms only of a favorite religion would result in scientific ideas being crushed and distorted to fit narrow preconceptions, while beautiful and apt imagery would be dismissed. We need to find those concepts that work, and only those, borrowing from many religions as well as other sources" (ibid.:8).

A mythologist can perhaps be forgiven for asking what would happen to the integrity of a particular traditional mythology. There is a striking disconnect between Primack and Abrams's rhetoric concerning the deep and beautiful imagery of traditional mythology and their sense of the world in which it existed. They comment in their discussion of classic Egyptian mythology, for example, "We don't want to return to the magic, superstition, and social horrors of the ancient world but to mine the good as best we can" (ibid.:47). The other side of partialness is amalgamation; Primack and Abram are universalists *and* multiculturalists, proceeding as though the new scientific universalism not only has room for but requires the input of diverse mythologies for the contributions they can make to scientific metaphor. But what if it turns out that some mythologies are highly useful for such metaphors, while others are of little use? Primack and Abrams are opening new grounds for comparative validation of different religions, based on their respective success in adumbrating science. Conceivably, a new religious one-upsmanship could ensue.

Traditional mythologies will be salvaged only partially in the Primack and Abrams project, and their role will change from that of authority to that of means: mythologies will become a tool useful for the new object of veneration—science. "A new science-based cosmology could be capable of centering a global community around a common consensus on what reality is and how it all came about" (ibid.:40). In sum: Primack and Abrams promise a colorful, varied, cosmopolitan mytho-pastiche, with hints of exoticism, re-purposed as science metaphor and in which the traditional authority, force, and integrity of mythological worlds have been diluted if not dismissed in favor of the authority and integrity of science.

A final point intriguing to any mythologist and frustrating to some is the significance Primack and Abrams, in their re-mythologizing program, accord to the late celebrity-mythologist Joseph Campbell (2004). As I noted in a different context (see chapter 3), the reliance on Campbell facilitates the dilution of mythology. In the context of scientific cosmology, there is an additional problem. Campbell follows a Jungian line of interpretation that approaches myth as though it is the psyche's autobiography, a recounting of the process of a generic human psyche maturing. Importantly, Campbell himself implies that one who reads mythology as cosmology is misreading it.[2] To the extent that Jungian-Campbellian symbolism is tapped for portraying cosmic process, the implication would seem to be that the growth of the human psyche mirrors the growth of the cosmos. Such an implication would obviously provide a useful route for re-envisioning the cosmos as our perfect home, but we have to ask whether Primack and Abrams's Campbellian inclinations might not lead into a kind of reading of myth that Campbell himself has warned against.

DAILY BREAD: A MODERN PARABLE

Primack and Abrams's cosmic program is like a "sensible" diet plan. We need a plan for emotional reintegration into the cosmos, in part at least for the same reason we need a new nutritional plan: specifically, that the modern world has rendered our once adaptive appetites obsolete. The craving for calorie-rich foods, which may have been adaptive in a life of physical exertion and the specter of food shortage, is now, in many parts of the world, maladaptive, as are pantheons of robust gods who used to provide psychological and sociological anchors but who now, so goes the claim, interfere with the benefits that derive from our attempts to understand the cosmos objectively. The obsolescence of our food-appetites, of course, is only one of several reasons adduced to account for our recent gains in girth; other, more specific factors include the rise of highly processed, engineered "food," the "culture of excess," a sedentary lifestyle, and new forms of psychological stress. But these more specific factors are themselves conditions made possible through science and technology; together they constitute the new context that pairs badly with our old appetites. Both of the problems, nutritional and cosmo-emotional, are thus, in part at least, negative side effects of benefits brought by scientific technologies: in one case, by improvements in food production and in machines that free us from the labor and limited food sources that once matched our appetites and, in the other, by observational instruments that have revealed false assumptions in our worldview spawned by our anthropocentric inclinations. Perhaps more important, the solutions to both problems are also steeped in the methods, measures, and mystique of science. Science confronting two problems it has created: on the surface the two problems are quite different, yet the proposed solutions are oddly convergent.[3]

There appear to be four basic strategies for dealing with our maladaptive appetites; these are summarized next. Two of them (the second and third) proceed from the assumption that in the modern world we *cannot* satisfy our antiquated natural desires, and two (the first and fourth) proceed from the assumption that we *can*.

The first is denial: to go on eating red meat and believing that the Earth is the center of a universe full of robust, emotionally satisfying gods who mimic and magnify our human quirks and personalities. Denial provides satisfaction but is not a healthy choice, and, on both levels, we should avoid it.

The second strategy is to attempt to modify the natural appetite itself, the most obvious method being mood-altering nutritional supplements or drugs (some are directed specifically toward cravings for food; I'm not aware of any directed specifically toward cosmic ennui). The prevailing wisdom is that these should be the last resort, invoked if the other strategies fail. This is reasonable, so only two alternatives are left.

The third is to bite the bullet: the "no pain, no gain" strategy that gave rise to a new form of asceticism in the 1980s, that of the lunch hour spent in the fitness center rather than the bistro. The cosmic equivalent is to just accept that "there is not much of comfort in any of this"—astrophysicist and Nobel laureate Steven Weinberg's words (1984:143–44), but there is a long tradition behind them (see Schrempp 2012a: chapter 6). The strategy is rooted in a sort of heroic extremism, which has several upsides: on the one hand, the intrinsic satisfaction, if not heroism, of taking an uncompromised stance; on the other, the fact that hunger can make our (restricted) food more satisfying. Weinberg's "little island of warmth and love" (see above) is the medieval monk's rapture at the simple, earnest architecture of his cell and his daily crust of bread and bowl of warm soup.[4] There are also downsides to "no pain, no gain." In the 1980s this body-management strategy was sometimes adopted as a personal microcosm of predatory capitalism: the lean, mean body that sought to locally and personally instantiate the economic-macrocosmic forces of the same. Asceticism has limits, most notably that self-denial is difficult to sustain through the long term, especially under conditions of modern stress, another component of the world we have created for ourselves.

The fourth and last strategy offers the fresh alternative of a "sensible" plan that, rooted in science, will surely appeal to the smart ones among us. Interestingly, Primack and Abrams came along about the time that "no pain, no gain" was on the decline and "sensible" diets were on the rise. The mainstay of the latter is to identify lighter, benign, or at least less harmful substitutes for the objects of one's now-maladaptive desires. Hence the great market for balanced, healthy meals, which one can purchase pre-measured and pre-prepared under such labels as Sensible Cuisine. These meals often contain elements from exotic cuisines to add appeal and interest. The faith is that freshness (usually a kind of processed freshness), variety, color, crunchiness, and creativity will provide alternatives to fat, "bad" cholesterol and other now-harmful substances. This food is to be accompanied by an otherwise healthy lifestyle that includes moderate rather than extreme exercise. Primack and Abrams give us the cosmic equivalent: science-rich but mytho-lite cosmic insights—such as that we exist at the temporal midpoint of cosmic expansion—along with partial, diluted, processed mythology as substitutes for the visceral centrality we have fed on in the past. Abstract, sophisticated, low-cholesterol cosmic fare replaces the old unruly, needy, polysaturated pantheons.

For those who accept science as the final authority on the cosmos but want to avoid cosmic anorexia, Primack and Abrams's plan may be the best and is certainly the most comprehensive now available. Unfortunately, and this is perhaps best viewed as one of the prices we pay for "progress" (so back to option three?), the Primack and Abrams plan will leave some with a question that is felt, if not voiced, after a meal of Sensible Cuisine: when do we eat?

NOTES

1. In *Faith and Reason*, a video documentary written and hosted by Margaret Wertheim (1998). Another famous summary comment by Weinberg, referring to the seeming point-lessness of the cosmos, is considered in chapter 7.

2. See especially Campbell (2004:237).

3. Perhaps the convergence is odd only from a scientific point of view. From the stand-point of traditional mythological cosmogonies, the problems of human appetite for cosmic home and for food are often closely related; consider, for example, the role of Demeter (agri-culture) in Hesiod's *Theogony*.

4. In some ways Weinberg's "island" converges with the satisfactions offered in the next strategy but is given a different effect through the context of extremism and asceticism in contrast to the spirit of moderation.

6

It's a Wonderfully Conflicted Life!
The Survival of Mythology in the Capra-Corn Cosmos

In the late 1950s, Frank Capra, the Hollywood filmmaker best known for *It's a Wonderful Life* and other depictions of optimistic Americana (aka "Capra-corn"), directed four popular science films with the sponsorship of Bell Telephone: *Our Mr. Sun* (1956), *Hemo the Magnificent* (1957), *The Strange Case of the Cosmic Rays* (1957), and *The Unchained Goddess* (1958). Although both the tape-analog and digital video-recording technologies we now take for granted were yet to come, countless children viewed these films in grade school through the primitive but treasured technology of the time: the clicking and sometimes smoking film projector. Capra claimed that the Bell System had 1,600 prints of each film in circulation (Gilbert 1997:223). Nominally for children, the hour-long films were also viewed by parents in highly publicized television broadcasts. In his autobiography, Capra (1997:443) says he made these films for "youngsters from eight to eighty." Like many programs of that time, especially cartoons (which these films used in abundance), the content could be read at different levels.

There is a good deal of mythological content in Capra's science films, but discussion of it has been largely eclipsed by interest in Capra's techniques for infusing his portrayal of science with religion—which, I argue, is not synonymous, at least in these films, with mythology. As a folkloristically oriented mythologist, I take exception to this neglect and will flesh out Capra's use of mythology and the strategies behind it. Chapter 5 explored a productive tension within the concept of myth itself—the fact that it designates both grand cosmogonic story and quotidian ideology. By contrast, this chapter explores the tensions between myth and two other big concepts that label modes of human engagement of the cosmos, namely, religion and science.

From the standpoint of mythology, Capra's science films are of interest for several reasons. The most obvious is that the characters that appear

DOI: 10.7330/9780874219708.c006

in these films are drawn from, or in some way (e.g., by dress or accoutrements) allude to, characters from mythology, especially Greek mythology. More abstractly, Capra's films exude a strong sense of formula and variation, a quality of great interest to students of both film and traditional oral narrative, evident in the influence on modern screenwriting of works by scholars who have endeavored to lay bare the underlying formulas of traditional oral narratives—Vladimir Propp (*The Morphology of the Folktale*) and Joseph Campbell (*The Hero with a Thousand Faces*) come especially to mind. But Capra's four science films are of interest to a mythologist for yet another reason. Specifically, these films about the nature of science are also about the nature of mythology, since they continually invoke the idea of myth as a foil against which to develop a vision of science. Capra employs both a dyadic myth-science contrast and a triadic contrast among myth, science, and religion. Shorn of the Capra charm, these schemata, I will argue, are models already familiar to folklorists in the social evolutionism of the nineteenth century, particularly in the work of E. B. Tylor. These models were created in the seventeenth and eighteenth centuries by the *philosophes* of the Enlightenment and were passed along by nineteenth-century social evolutionist thinkers, whence they were tapped by nineteenth- and twentieth-century popular science writers seeking to tell the heroic story of science. From there they departed for Hollywood, swept along in the great mid-twentieth-century West Coast brain-drain.

Analysis of Capra's films will be in two parts. First I consider them from the standpoint of formula and variation, noting the mythological influences on characters and plots. Second, I offer a synthesis, drawn from the films, of Capra's views about the relation of myth and science and of these to the third entity important to Capra and his audience—religion. Along the way I also consider another issue. Even though Capra's films may seem too up-front to allow for much self-parody, a self-reflexive commentary inheres in the very nature of the performer-audience relation in these films. Specifically, "Dr. Research" and "Mr. Fiction Writer"—two characters played by actual humans—are throughout making their case to two audiences: a group of cartoon characters appearing in these films (produced through pre-computerized studio animation), on one hand, and, on the other, the home viewing audience. The animated cartoon "people" in effect offer the home audience an opportunity to watch itself react to the idea of science. I call attention to instances in which Capra employs this circumstance to portray his sense of the nature of the home audience and his strategies for convincing it of his message.

***

The discussion that follows is organized in terms of three dimensions of formula: frame (or setting), antagonists (or characters), and plot and lesson (or plot and denouement). I first characterize these aspects in terms of qualities common to all four films—the grand formula—and then consider each film as a particular variation on it.

THE GRAND FORMULA

Frame: The setting is a film-production studio in which two characters played by actual humans, Dr. Research and Mr. Fiction Writer, are deliberating (in three films, about a science education program they are planning/rehearsing; in the fourth, about a literary prize). In the course of the deliberations these actual humans dialogue with "people" who are produced through techniques of "animation," either cartoons or puppets. Hereafter the "animated" figures (whether cartoons or puppets) will be referred to as "animateds."[1] The term *animation* has an interesting resonance with *animism*—treating the lifeless as though alive—which for many nineteenth-century mythologists was all but synonymous with "mythology."

Antagonists: Dr. Research (played by Dr. Frank Baxter) has great knowledge of science; he is also wise and idealistically committed to it. Mr. Fiction Writer (Eddie Albert in the first film, Richard Carlson for the others) is also committed to science but is less knowledgeable, more prone to youthful enthusiasm, and impetuous. He also sometimes grows impatient with the animateds (who are his artistic creations), calling them by derogatory nicknames until Dr. Research, the elder statesman, intervenes. Dr. Research is the philosopher and scientist,[2] Mr. Fiction Writer is the artist.

For three of the films (*Mr. Sun*, *Hemo*, and *Goddess*) the main animateds are cartoon figures either based on mythology (especially Greek mythology) or created to seem like figures from mythology (e.g., Hemo [Blood] is a heroic-looking figure in toga-like garb). Their organization reflects sociopolitical structures that are pre-modern (based on kinship, kingship, and the paternalism of noblesse oblige). These animateds represent the aspects of nature to be explored and are continually juxtaposed to photographic images of the realms of nature they represent (the animated Mr. Sun is juxtaposed to photographs of the actual sun, Hemo to microscopic photographs of arteries, blood cells, and so on). Rather than cartoon figures based on nature mythology, the animateds in *Cosmic Rays* are puppets of three literary figures (created by Bil and Cora Baird Marionettes): Edgar Allen Poe, Charles Dickens, and Fyodor Dostoevsky. All of the animateds in all of the films are of romantic temperament and initially resistant, if not hostile, to the cause of science. The films encourage a degree of ambiguity and audience suspension of disbelief regarding the animateds: on one hand, the animateds are presented as the creation of Mr. Fiction Writer; on the other hand, they invariably take on a life of their own.

Plot and lesson: The basic plot (or in Propp's famous formula, the "lack/lack liquidated") is that the animateds initially resist the cause of science but are then converted to it. This basic plot gives rise to colorful rhetoric, strategies, subplots, and showdowns. Accompanying the conversion of the animateds are inspirational messages: science is noble; science and religion mutually support one another; God has given only humans the mind to pursue science, and it is part of his plan that they do so.

VARIATIONS ON THE FORMULA

Our Mr. Sun (1956)

Frame: Mr. Fiction Writer uses the studio screen to present mockups of Mr. Sun and Father Time for a proposed science film about the sun, but the mockups come to life on their own.

Antagonists: The two main animateds in this film, Mr. Sun and Father Time, parallel the human dyad of Dr. Research and Mr. Fiction Writer. Father Time, like Dr. Research, is older and more philosophical; Mr. Sun, like Mr. Fiction Writer, is younger (a curmudgeon, but less so than Father Time), more impetuous and artistic (indeed, Mr. Sun will himself become a screenwriter/film director [see below]). Dyads are familiar in the world of television, especially in sportscasting and talk shows; but colorful pairs of characters—one typically more sober, the other more playful, and often taking the form of twins (*dioscori*)—are also familiar figures in traditional mythologies.

Plot and lesson: Mr. Sun, claiming he should be the director, presents his own version of how the film should go (giving us a film within a film). Mr. Sun's proposed film opens with him intoning a poem that amounts to an inversion of St. Francis's thirteenth-century *Canticle to the Sun* recast from the sun's point of view: the sun greeting earth dwellers as family members rather than humans greeting the sun and the rest of nature as family members (the *Canticle* will be referenced again at the end as Dr. Research recites the sun's benefits for humanity). Mr. Sun calls attention to the reverence and affection toward him displayed in pre-scientific mythico-religious traditions. A parade of anthropomorphic images from these traditions passes in review; Mr. Sun approves of these portrayals of him, though he adds that many people had "some pretty odd notions" about him. Mr. Sun ends his film (i.e., the film within the film) by venting his vexation: science wants to end all of this and portray him instead as "a big blob of mass holding little blobs of mass together with gravity instead of with love." Through the remainder of the film (i.e., the larger film), Dr. Research, aided by Mr. Fiction Writer, convinces Mr. Sun that science will not destroy human reverence for, or personal connection with, nature; science emerges as a noble enterprise.

Hemo the Magnificent (1957)

Frame: The frame is largely similar to *Mr. Sun*, featuring the studio and the "magic screen"—identified with Mr. Fiction Writer's creative imagination. Dr. Research and Mr. Fiction Writer are at work on another film, this time about blood and circulation.

Antagonists: The animated Hemo consists of a human form inscribed over a valentine-shaped heart of red and blue (arterial and venous) blood. Hemo does not seem to be based on any specific figure from mythology, yet, partly because of his toga and his association with nature, he would blend in with other figures from Greek mythology. Instead of a dyad of animateds (as in *Mr. Sun*), the animateds here can be described as a "gang" with a leader (Capra had in fact worked briefly on the *Our Gang* film/television series). Specifically, Hemo, a symbol of blood (and more generally of life), runs around in the forest with the gang of devoted animals—including a turtle, rabbit, deer, alligator, and others. Although lovable, they are dimwitted—distinctly "yokels." Hemo is their hero and protector; at one point they refer to him as their "king."

The film opens with a planning session in progress for an upcoming film. Hemo's gang of cartoon animal characters appears on the magic screen, and Dr. Research and Mr. Fiction Writer chat with them, mentioning that they are planning a film about "Hemo the Magnificent." Alarmed, a bird flies off to tell Hemo, who appears and tells the humans that he does not want them to make his story since, for humans, blood represents "disease, wounds, pain" or "a smear on a slide," while his animal friends know the truth: blood is "health, life." Hemo says his story should be told by "poets" rather than scientists. Dr. Research tells Hemo that humans seek truth through many avenues, one of which is science, and Hemo agrees to give him a chance; like Mr. Sun, he is ultimately won over.

In addition to this human-size Hemo who runs around with forest animals, a central role is played by a group of diminutive men who illustrate the workings of internal organs in the circulation of blood. A little man in a business suit ("Mr. Big") sits in a room that represents the upper part of the human brain; he monitors inputs and, through phone lines, sends directives to other little men distributed throughout the body, including a team of minuscule myocardial musclemen in gym clothes who push rubber squeeze bulbs to move the blood. This set of little men is used to illustrate changes in blood circulation in various scenarios. For example, in a prize-fight scene, they illustrate loss of consciousness. As one boxer takes a punch, a "dispatcher" (a little man at a switchboard in the lower brain) takes a spill and passes out. As a result, the management of blood flow to different parts of the body goes unattended. Too little blood reaches the upper brain, so Mr. Big passes out in the monitoring room and fails to send the proper directives; as a result, the fighter loses consciousness and topples over.

Plot and lesson: After listening to the scientific discourse for awhile, Hemo, unimpressed, beckons his animal friends to depart; but Dr. Research asks, "Mr. Turtle, have you ever seen your heart?" and shows him a clip of a turtle's beating heart. He shows other animals clips of their hearts, and they become absorbed in what science has to say, as though the success of science will depend on an appeal to audience self-absorption. The appeal of science is that it shows us ourselves. What captures the hearts, so to speak, of the animals thus offers a mirror image of the film's strategy: the animateds entranced by realistic footage are the inverse of real people entranced by studio animation.

Hemo is wearied because Dr. Research focuses on the mechanics of circulation ("plumbing") rather than on (in Hemo's terms) "who I am." Hemo throws out a challenge: he will continue to listen only if Dr. Research is able to adduce the "two key words" that most capture "the poetry, the mystery, and the true meaning of blood" and that most connect blood to "the mystical origins and traditions of life." To the astonishment of Mr. Fiction Writer and the guffaws of the animals, Dr. Research answers "seawater." Hemo announces that the answer is correct, apologizes to Dr. Research, and bids Dr. Research to recount what science has found out about blood. The account continues with an evolutionary origin of blood chemistry from seawater ("in the beginning Hemo was the sea"). The scene is a fascinating attempt to imbue the perspective of biological evolutionism with a quasi-religious sense of cosmic unity, mystery, and awe. In the end, the animals want to be scientists, but Hemo gently tells them that science is only for humans.

The Strange Case of the Cosmic Rays (1957)

Frame: Mr. Fiction Writer's imagination—the "magic screen"—comes to life with a newscast of a throng of spectators. An on-the-scene reporter describes what is happening: the spectators are surrounding a building in which Edgar Allen Poe, Charles Dickens, and Fyodor Dostoevsky are deciding the winner of this year's "Edgar" prize for the best mystery story of the first half of the twentieth century. All the figures in the newscast scene—spectators, the newsman, and literary figures—are cleverly done puppets that subtly caricature real-life people (realistically enough that, while making this film, Capra reportedly started to give them directions).[3] Dr. Research and Mr. Fiction Writer interrupt the judges' deliberations and present the research on cosmic rays of the previous half-century as a late-arriving submission to the mystery contest.

Antagonists: The newscast scene, and particularly the room with the three judges, is returned to repeatedly throughout the film, as the humans debate with the judges of the literary contest. The film is about the discovery of cosmic rays, a quest portrayed as beginning with a scientific experiment that demonstrated that an unknown, mysterious force—a "phantom bandit"—"robs" charged objects of electrons (the force will turn out to be cosmic rays). Two additional groups of animateds (in both cases, cartoons) are employed prominently in the film to portray this scenario of thievery and the search for the culprit. One is a set of "Wild West" figures (bank robbers, a sheriff, and so on). The other is Fagin and his "henchmen," the gang of thieves and their ringleader from Dickens's *Oliver Twist* (Fagin is an atom stripped of electrons, cast off by stars to form cosmic rays; these "Fagins" produce other "henchmen" particles when they enter the Earth's atmosphere). Although stemming from literature rather than myth, Fagin's gang is reminiscent of Hemo's (or Meteora's [see below]); the animated Fagin-and-gang, periodically juxtaposed to scientific evidence of cosmic rays, are used to illustrate the processes thought to govern the latter.

Plot and lesson: Since this science story involves the search for a thief, the humans interrupt the deliberations of the literary judges and try to persuade them that the scientific search for the electron-thieving force should get the "Edgar" for best mystery story. The deeper question that underlies all four films—is science good—is thus, in the mystery story context, given an additional valence: is science captivating? Indeed, the usual plot line of science proving to be important is paralleled by a subplot in *Cosmic Rays* in which Dostoevsky, initially pronouncing science "a big bore," comes to be smitten by it. Finally and most abstractly, through the discussions between the humans (Dr. Research and Mr. Fiction Writer) and the animateds (the judges of the literary contest) runs a question that is still deeply implicated in the venture of popular science: does science offer a *story*?

The literary and real-life (or romanticized real-life) source of the animateds in *Cosmic Rays* contrasts with the mythological source of the animateds in the other three films. The difference perhaps reflects the nature of the specific topic; unlike the sun, blood, and weather, cosmic rays are invisible and lack a perceivable relationship to ordinary human experience. It is perhaps for this reason that they are without prototypes in traditional mythologies. It is perhaps also for the same reason—the distance from ordinary experience—that the topic of this particular film, particle physics, raises the question of why ordinary people should be interested in science. At one point a despondent Dostoevsky asks what's in science for "common people who work, love, hate."

Although the judges, by the end of the film, are clearly convinced of the cause of science, they cannot resolve their literary dilemma: can they give the prize to a story that is "unfinished"? Dickens proposes a creative solution: the scientists will be invited back in another fifty years to tell us what "new chapters they've added to their cosmic tale." Thus, although the basic message of the value of science comes through clearly, the conclusion embodies a note of plot ambiguity absent from the first two films, in service of the message that science is an ongoing, unfinished venture whose ultimate end is, in Dostoevsky's words, solving the mystery of "creation itself."

The Unchained Goddess (1958)

Frame: As in *Cosmic Rays*, the opening scene of *Unchained Goddess* lies outside the film studio; indeed, the film's opening recalls that of Capra's *It's a Wonderful Life* (in which the angel-in-training, Clarence, is briefed for an intervention into the human world as envisioned from a "god's-eye view"). *Goddess* opens with realistically photographed clouds swirling as an imperial female voice proclaims:

> Like to see something amusing? In a moment two men, a scientist and a writer, are going to rehearse a weather program.
> The story of Weather, they call it. But what do humans know of weather? *I* am Weather—I Meteora, Goddess of Weather . . . Let's watch them make fools of themselves.

The scene shifts to the film studio, arranged to look like a weather station, where Mr. Fiction Writer is telling Dr. Research about his difficulty coming up with a concept for this film. The studio screen is said to be his imagination, and it is blank. When robust laughter is heard from the screen, the filmmaker says his imagination must be coming up with something.

Antagonists: Again we have the dyad of Dr. Research and Mr. Fiction Writer, although their tone in the debates with the animateds is noticeably more aggressive—more heady and self-congratulatory regarding human progress in science—than in the previous films. Dr. Research and Mr. Fiction Writer hear laughter from the magic screen, and then a set of cartoon gods of the weather appears on it. They are:

- Meteora, human in form, except the stylized evening gown she is wearing continues downward to (and seemingly past) the edge of the screen.
- Cirrus, a cartoon caricature of a painter who creates clouds with his pallet and brush.
- Boreas, wind god, a cloud shape with minimalistically imposed human facial features.
- A trio of weather gods, three stylized little men who produce rain, snow, and hail (respectively from a watering can, bowl, and peashooter); they sometimes stand on top of one another in "totem pole" fashion.
- Thor, in Viking garb wielding a hammer and lightning bolts, appears at a later point.

Reminiscent of Hemo and his gang of animals or Fagin and his gang, the weather gods are humbly submissive to Meteora. Portrayed on the studio screen, they are apparently hovering up in the air, as no platform (or indeed any other orienting structure) appears on the screen along with them. Meteora too is hovering; her gown continues downward to the edge of the screen, and neither feet nor a hem ever appear.

Plot and lesson: The question of whether science is good (*Mr. Sun, Hemo*) takes on, in *Cosmic Rays*, added coloration—is science interesting—and metamorphoses, in *Unchained Goddess*, into yet another query: does science work? Can science predict and control the weather?

The debate between the humans and animateds concerns the "real" cause of weather, and the arguments are directed toward Meteora. The humans put forward the scientific explanations, while Meteora's minion-gods present themselves as the real cause. Recalling but reversing the "sea-water" challenge of *Hemo*, this time Dr. Research precipitates the show-down. He holds a candle up to the screen and challenges Meteora's minions: "Neither rain nor snow nor sleet shall still this flame." Meteora ups the ante by offering to marry the god who puts the candle out. After all the minion gods fail, Dr. Research succeeds. Meteora turns against her minions, calling them "charlatans"—thus inverting the "popular revolt" depicted in *Hemo*, in which Dr. Research succeeds in turning the attention of the minions, the forest animals, away from their "king."

To the now-attentive Meteora, Dr. Research and Mr. Fiction Writer explain the progress that has been made in understanding weather processes and in prediction. The metaphor underlying their exposition is that of a psychiatric clinic staffed by "weather psychiatrists" dedicated to understanding the moods of a female patient; the metaphor draws from several trends of the 1950s, including a public fascination with psychoanalysis, the inscrutability and deviousness of the feminine as a popular theme in film, and the fact that all hurricanes at the time were branded as female (only female names were used for hurricanes until 1979). Different weather patterns are analogized to Meteora's different moods; Mr. Fiction Writer refers to hurricanes, for example, as "your all-out two-week tantrums." After hearing the scientific analysis of hurricanes, Meteora replies, innocently, "This is beyond anything I ever dreamed of. Even in my vilest moods you still understand me." Boreas then asks, "Anybody know the address of the old gods' home" (a variation on "old folks' home," a term since superseded by "senior care facility" and other terms). Recalling that Hemo's animal friends wanted to be scientists, the minion weather gods wonder whether there might be work for them in the clinic.

As the humans elaborate on the progress of science, Meteora swoons and shifts from her imperious voice to a Marilyn Monroe–innocence inflection. Amid footage on various kinds of storms she says, "It's such a lovely warm feeling, Mr. Scientist, to be understood, even when I'm temperamental."

The minions have lost heart. Her minion gods having failed her, Meteora proposes marriage to Dr. Research, who at one point appears through her eyes dressed as Homer. Professing that he is already married, Dr. Research lets her down gently.

After inspirational monologues by Dr. Research about science, Mr. Fiction Writer, recalling that the weather report was for clear skies, opens the curtains; it is pouring. Affairs of the heart between mortals and gods are common in traditional mythologies; thus a viewer might leap to the conclusion that the rain is Meteora's tears. But the gods laugh uproariously, and Meteora says coyly to a blushing Dr. Research, "Thank you, Mr. Scientist, it *was* amusing." The comment recalls the lines she spoke to open the film, and the scene rapidly changes to another scenario familiar in mythologies: the gods have been toying with us humans all along.

The conclusion suggests an ambiguity, one much larger than that of *Cosmic Rays*. The gods appearing on the screen identified with Mr. Fiction Writer's imagination implies that these gods are his own creation. But in the film's opening and closing lines, the gods can be seen as having final control (including control of Mr. Fiction Writer's imagination; this would amount to a more distant version of Mr. Sun taking over the making of his own film). The situation has an intriguing resonance with a theme found in modern thinkers—including Freud, Marx, and Durkheim—but that is actually quite a lot older: that humans invent gods out of fear and ignorance and then allow these phantoms of their own devising to shape human consciousness and control human life. In notable contrast to the other films, the humans' confidence in the achievements of science in *Goddess* initially verges on boastfulness. At the very least, the film has fun with the classic theme of *hubris*—and what better topic than the "art" of weather prediction? This quality is emboldened by the situation of men showing off in front of a woman. Meteora is a lone female goddess between the sparring male humans and gods, a scenario that resonates with the *Iliad* (Homer 1989). Indeed, early in the film Meteora boasts of the decisive effect she can have on history with the example of the Spanish Armada; she is, so to speak, the face that sank a thousand ships.

At this point, several additional details can be added to the general formula uniting the four films.

Laughter: In all four films, the animateds, initially resistant to science, laugh at the scientists. In each case the laughter is very colorful and takes a form unique to the particular film. In *Mr. Sun*, the laughter is that of a pair of curmudgeons (Mr. Sun and Father Time). In *Hemo* the laughter, with Hemo's encouragement, comes from the animals that follow Hemo; it is the ignorant guffawing of yokels.[4] In *Cosmic Rays*, the laughter, initially coming from an indeterminate source (appropriate to the mystery story format), is the stereotyped evil laugh of the villain in a melodrama. In *Goddess*, the laughter is the robust belly laughs of gods who are pranksters.

Family portraits of wonder: Each film has a moment when the animateds, initially resistant to science, suddenly become intrigued. Each group of animateds—Mr. Sun and Father Time, Hemo and the animals, the three puppet judges of the mystery story contest, Meteora and her minions—looks out at the scientists (or is it to the home audience?) in a state of innocent, transfixed wonder, forming a harmonious family portrait. The portrait also projects an idealized vision of the family viewing audience. This particular moment, more than any overt action, conveys the reality of a "formula" uniting the four films; perhaps it is Capra's attempt to portray the glimpse of the eternal that he held as an article of faith (discussed later). The conversion to recognition of the value of science comes rather suddenly, allowing a dramatic thawing of the coldness: the puppet Dostoevsky is the best example, as he metamorphoses from world-weary and brooding to enchanted and warm, but a similar dramatic transformation is found in each of the main animateds.

Music: As was typical of Hollywood's "Golden Age," the background music is mostly classical. Beethoven figures with special prominence, the choral "Ode to Joy" from the Ninth Symphony providing the background to the inspirational messages in the closing sections of all but *Goddess* (in which the inspirational closing transpires a little earlier, allowing for the final impish twist: the gods' having us on).[5] The music adds a feeling of heightened fantasy to some scenes: Meteora's appearance is often accompanied by a velvety "I Dream of Jeanie" (which Capra had also tapped for the lead female in *Mr. Smith Goes to Washington*); a parade of mythical representations of the sun in *Mr. Sun* is accompanied by Berlioz's *Symphonie Fantastique* (which the composer claimed was based on a mad dream); the more turbulent weather scenes in *Goddess* are accompanied by the rousing, mythologically inspired music of Wagner.

Showdowns: There is a long and rich tradition of showdowns in myth and legend. Those in the Capra science films at some moments call to mind the showdown between Moses vs. the Pharaoh's magicians in their competing claims to posses cosmic power and at other times the folk hero "John Henry," since these films put tremendous emphasis on technical scientific apparatus (telescopes, computers, balloons, and rockets carrying scientific instruments aloft) as the key that unlocks the secrets of the universe. Hemo and Mr. Sun specifically disparage this cold, monstrous technology but are won over by the noble aims propelling it.

MYTHOLOGY IN THE CAPRA-CORN COSMOS

The ostensible point of these films is to explain science; but in striving for this goal they also convey, indirectly, a number of ideas and attitudes about an entity with which science is repeatedly contrasted—namely, mythology. It is striking how intricate the view of myth is, given the seeming simplicity of the vehicle. Relying mainly on the films themselves, I will draw out the implicit commentary on the place of myth in the Capra-corn cosmos. Though the view of myth presented is what might be called the standard popular science view—a heroic story of science's triumph over myth and superstition—Capra's is one of the cleverest and subtlest, and clearly the most charming, renditions of this view.

But it is important to note that in these films Capra, in the end, juxtaposes not two but three human frameworks for understanding the cosmos: myth, science, and religion. James Gilbert (1997) provides an informative and subtle analysis of these films, but he does so as though Capra's strategy and project inhere in the relation of just those two entities: religion and science. I, too, am inclined to look for a contrast between two opposed entities, but, given my predispositions as a mythologist, I tend to look for it in the well-worn formula of a great divide between myth and science (rather than religion and science). *Mythology* and *religion* as terms are often used nearly synonymously, and that is part of the problem. In the course of my research, I have had to conclude that mythology and religion, as presented in these films, are two different things and that, to elaborate on the role of mythology for Capra, the roles of all three (including the three permutations of two contained within them) must ultimately be considered.

The view of mythology presented by Capra is the more or less standard view one encounters nowadays in popular science; the basic principles of this view, in turn, were laid down in the eighteenth-century philosophical movement of the Enlightenment. Eighteenth-century doctrines about myth were passed to nineteenth-century social thinkers who presented them as integral to the social evolutionist doctrines of that era. Although now disso- ciated from many of the broader connotations of social evolutionism, these doctrines still play a central role in many contemporary portrayals of the growth of science, particularly in the portrayals offered in popular science (see Schrempp 2012a:25–26).

Among the ideas about myth commonly endorsed by thinkers of the Enlightenment are these:[6]

1. Mythology originated in archaic conditions of ignorance and fear.

2. Archaic myths sought to explain the forces of nature by analogy to what was known in the first stage of knowledge; this meant that mythic ex- planation was highly anthropomorphic, portraying natural processes as the consequence of the actions of humanlike gods. For example, in *Of the Ori- gin of Fables*, Bernard Fontenelle wrote: "One had often seen water poured out of a pitcher. One could then imagine with ease how a god could pour out the water of a river; and by the same facility one had in imagining it, one was completely moved to believe it. Thus, to give a reason for thunder and lightning, one could willingly picture to oneself a god in human form throwing arrows of fire at us—ideas manifestly taken from very familiar objects" (Fontenelle 1975 [1724]:11–12).

3. Since myth arose as an attempt to explain nature, its project amounts to an inferior version of the project of science; eventually, myth will be su- perseded by science.

4. The key shift that marks the passage from mythology to science is the shift from anthropomorphic explanation to explanation through the workings of impersonal natural laws.

5. It is in some peoples' interest to exploit the masses' love of mythology and keep them in ignorance. Coteries of priests duping the masses with mythology formed a mainspring of archaic society.

6. Ignorance is not the only source of the human attraction to mythology, for the mental life of the ordinary individual is parochial and self-absorbed and for that reason, too, inclined toward mythology over science.

7. Religion lies somewhere between mythology and science.

The final point admitted a number of variations. At one end of a continuum, religion was, for some Enlightenment thinkers, barely distinguishable from mythology. At the other end of the continuum were thinkers who argued that religion is a distinct form but that it shares some characteristics with myth (notably a belief in person-like forces operating in the universe) and other characteristics with science (notably abstraction, rigor, and systematicity). In *The Natural History of Religion*, David Hume wrote: "It seems certain that, according to the natural progress of human thought, the ignorant multitude must first entertain some groveling and familiar notion of superior powers, before they stretch their conception to that perfect Being, who bestowed order on the whole frame of nature. We may as reasonably imagine, that men inhabited palaces before huts and cottages, or studied geometry before agriculture; as assert that the Deity appeared to them in a pure spirit, omniscient, omnipotent, and omnipresent, before he was apprehended to be a powerful, though limited being, with human passions and appetites, limbs and organs" (Hume 2008 [1757]:135–36).

In addition, divine revelation was sometimes adduced as distinguishing religion from mythology, and this revelation was often attributed to a rational Creator who designed a universe fit for science. The idea of religion forming a separate stage of human knowledge between mythology and science fit nicely with the popularity of three as the number of major epochs in the evolution of human knowledge, a preference that, in turn, perhaps instances a broader Western cultural attachment to threes (see Dundes 1968). E. B. Tylor, heir to the Enlightenment, set the tone for the anthropological study of mythology in the late nineteenth century; and the analysis in his *Primitive Culture* (1871) is riddled with tension between a three-way and a two-way contrast. On the one hand, there are three great epochs—myth-cum-magic, religion, and science—in Tylor's scheme of the evolution of human thought; on the other hand, his portrayal of the dynamics of this evolution revolves around a struggle between only two principles: "animism" (belief in spiritual beings) and materialism (belief in impersonal laws of nature).[7]

Now, let us consider these themes in Capra's films, starting with the idea of a shift from personal to impersonal causation as the critical transition marking the origin of science. This theme is found throughout the Capra films, perhaps most pointedly in the crisis that precipitates Meteora's turning again her minions. Specifically, Boreas and Mr. Fiction Writer debate the "real" cause of wind. Boreas offers a personalized explanation: "I blow to please Meteora." Mr. Fiction Writer counters, "That's not why you blow, Windy . . . The real cause of Wind is the Sun." What follows is a scientific explanation of wind, based on diagrams and realistic photographs (although even this is punctuated with moments of anthropomorphic analogy, including a brief cameo view of the character "Mr. Sun"). When Meteora's minions fail to blow out the candle, Dr. Research comforts her with a statement about the origin of mythological deities: "Don't blame your gods, Meteora; they've been very real to us, even though we created them to hide our fears of the unknown."

The human attraction to mythology—the preference for mythological over scientific explanation, even to the point of a readiness to be duped—permeates Capra's films, which, in effect, project these inclinations onto nature itself. Meteora adores Homer's account of her; the animal-yokels adore the mythic Hemo, and Mr. Sun says that the portrayal of him that he likes best is the Greeks' portrayal of Phoebus-Apollo: "Apollo racing across the sky in his fiery chariot, making heavenly music on his golden ukulele, oh, that was for me, I loved it! And then along came another Greek to spoil it all, a Greek who would rather think than worship sun gods. Anaxagoras was his name."

The other part of the equation, the existence of humans ready to dupe those who are ready to be duped, also appears: it is Hemo who, despite his benign intentions, most epitomizes the manipulative priest. He is presented as having known the truth of science all along and as having indulged the animals and kept them innocent, although he is also protecting them. When the animals find out about science and ask if they can be scientists, he faces the hard tasking of telling them that only humans can be scientists: "Friends, you might as well know it; the magic of knowledge and reasoning is only for humans."

But for Capra, if mythology stands in the way of science, it also offers a means of persuading the viewer that the transition is desirable. This recognition of myth's effectiveness as a lure is a tribute to its power, and Capra himself is the priest-manipulator wielding this power. Capra provides his newly minted mythological characters to urge viewers toward, and provide models of, the transformation to a scientific view. It is strategic appeals to our vanity—to the human self-absorption that promoted the original creation of mythology—that will win converts away from it. Dr. Research's appeal to Mr. Turtle, asking him whether he would like to see his own heart, is a microcosm of the film's intended effect on the TV audience. A calculated appeal to vanity can lead us to raise ourselves out of some of its parochializing effects.

At its worst, popular science is capable of the mythological mesmerizing the philosophers of the Enlightenment scorned: a self-proclaimed elite conjuring up pabulum to gratify the parochial, self-absorbed masses while consolidating their own prestige as rulers. In most instances of science popularization, however, the motives are more complex. The dilemma in Capra's films is endemic to the popularizing of science in general, since some of the most effective means of popularizing are not only non-scientific but antiscientific. Even though they are the most blatantly mythologized of popular science presentations, Capra's films are, from one point of view, just for that reason among the least blameworthy on the charge of duping the public—precisely because the mythologizing is blatant and unmistakable. In his films, one cannot mistake the fictional luring device for the scientifically envisioned "real"; indeed, one is constantly reminded of the distinction, sometimes quite unsubtly. Hemo is repeatedly juxtaposed with photographs of blood vessels and circulatory organs, Mr. Sun with astronomical photographs of the sun and stars, Meteora with weather instruments and footage of tornadoes and hurricanes. Vigilance toward the strategies of popular science is of greater necessity precisely when the mythologizing is *not* obvious (see Schrempp 2012a:9–11).

***

In Capra's films, the mythological gods undergo a diminishment (that, in the context of more refined art talk, might elicit the term *Götterdämmerung*) in culmination of the classic struggle: gods and humans each trying to control the other. Yet rather than confine them to scorn or oblivion, Dr. Research is careful to create an honorary place for the newly retired gods (*dei otiosi*). Near the end of *Unchained Goddess* Dr. Research says, "Without air and water, which are weather [he gestures toward Meteora, while Boreas bows to her], man would never have appeared on this small planet earth."

So, although her minion gods have been proven to be charlatans, Meteora is appeased and allowed, if ambiguously, to be "real." Given that the minions represent specific mechanisms of weather, the film's recommendation seems to be something like this: mythology, insofar as it proposes actual mechanisms of weather process, must be discarded; but mythology can still provide endearing symbols of the general phenomenon of weather and its human impact. An analogous reduction—from divine causality to human affection—occurs, more tersely, in *Mr. Sun* when Dr. Research says to Mr. Sun, "We used to worship you as an unknown god, but now that we know you better, we love you as our great and good friend."

What is mythology reduced *to*? The short answer is: art. Shorn of scientific and religious claims, mythology enters a realm in which fictional creations are nevertheless recognized as capturing, entertainingly, important human experiences: the beauty of nature, the fragility of the human condition, the moral danger of hubris. Hence Mr. Fiction Writer is the necessary associate of Dr. Research. The earlier mentioned nineteenth-century anthropologist-mythologist E. B. Tylor adumbrated Capra's understanding of the situation with the formula that archaic humans believed literally, and therefore erroneously, in the same figures that "civilized" peoples now enjoy as art. The fact that mythology, in three of the films, undergoes a reduction to art suggests why one does not sense a great discrepancy in the fact that the characters in the remaining film (*Cosmic Rays*) are drawn from literature rather than mythology; indeed, in the modern academy mythology is typically housed, along with other artistic "fiction," within departments of literature. The contrast that emerges here is in part the "analytical" vs. "artistic" brain; and, as noted, each of these two "sides" of the brain is given appropriate representation in Capra's film. Dr. Research (i.e., science) is the authority on the brain in those instances in which it is presented as a system of interrelated functions that maintain the life of the body (each function represented by a little man [see above]), a method that has a serious counterpart in artificial intelligence (AI) research.[8] By contrast, when Mr. Fiction Writer talks about the creative process in his own brain, he invokes standard art-talk tropes, directing them toward his "magic screen": it is blank at first, then suddenly its contents appear out of nowhere and take on a life of their own—to the point that he must contend with and rein in the creations of his own screen-imagination.

More problematic than the relation of mythology and science in Capra's science films is the relationship between mythology and religion. Religion (dominantly Judaeo-Christian, though there are ecumenical overtures to other contemporary major world religions) figures importantly in these films, as though the decline of myth leaves a spiritual void to be filled. Repeatedly citing the contributions of scientists from different parts of the world, Capra emphasizes the world-unifying character and potential of science; but through illustrations from several major world religions, he simultaneously suggests a world spiritual convergence around pan-human values, one of which, the films argue, should be science. If the relation of science to myth is one of displacement, the relation of science to religion is one of complementarity. In his autobiography and in these films, Capra projects a staunch dualism: there is a world of matter to be explored through science and a distinct world of spirit that transcends yet energizes the scientific enterprise. This duality is reflected in a number of related polarities as well, including body vs. mind and human vs. animal (science is only for the former). The dualism comes through clearly in the religious inspirational messages that close each film; in *Mr. Sun,* for example, Dr. Research tells Mr. Fiction Writer, worried that science will devalue humans, "You have a human spirit that separates you entirely from the animal world" and refers to the body as a "temple of the spirit." The emphasis in *Goddess* on new weather computers that can draw their own maps is accompanied by an equal emphasis on the fact that the computers must be primed by humans.

But Capra's dualism allows for equally robust moments of convergence between science and religion, especially in the culminating moments of the films. In the closing moments of *Hemo,* Max Planck is quoted regarding the necessity of "faith," while the Apostle Paul is quoted regarding the necessity to "prove all things." Above the images of these two figures appears the word *HOPE.*[9] Such gestures were not invented by Capra, nor did they end with him; writing in *Time* magazine about the recent evidence from the Large Hadron Collider confirming the "Higgs boson"—the so-called God particle—Jeffrey Kluger (2012:35) concludes: "We stopped for a moment to contemplate something far, far bigger than ourselves. And when that happened, faith and physics—which don't often shake hands—shared an embrace." Near the end of Capra's *Goddess,* the book of Job is quoted: "Hath the rain a Father? Or who hath begotten the drops of dew?" Derived from the Bible and yet asking about causality in nature, the passage is held up as an example of the spirit of curiosity shared by religion and science. In the culminating moments of *Cosmic Rays,* Dr. Research says, "The more we know of creation, the closer we get to the Creator." A sense of convergence is also aided by gestures toward the human convergence with the matter of the cosmos, for example, in the comment (noted earlier) that Hemo was originally the sea or the final line in *Cosmic Rays,* which, in the form of a concluding toast offered by Dickens, acknowledges the influence on human life of the particles or "celestial messengers" cast off by stars: "Three cheers for stardust."

But just what is the difference, for Capra, between religion and the other entity, mythology? In these films Capra never directly juxtaposes mythology and religion (as he does mythology and science). As noted, eighteenth-century philosophers, the source of the view of myth Capra represents, often did not clearly differentiate myth and religion, seeing them as overlapping or even identical in principle. For some, mythology was naive or childish religion; for others, talking about mythology offered a camouflaged way of talking about religion; while for yet others, interposing religion was a means of offering the public a "halfway house" for those not quite ready to make the transition from myth to science. But if Capra, too, avoids clarifying the relationship between myth and religion, it is for the opposite reason: clarification is unnecessary since in his mind they are *obviously* different. Religion, in Capra's science films, implies noble feelings about the existence of a God ultimately responsible for the cosmos, who has shared his nature uniquely with humans. Capra finds such noble ideas in Judaeo-Christian and other contemporary major world religions; he does not find them (and, more important, does not look for them) in Greek or other "mythologies," which are left as failed attempts to understand nature. He does not locate (or look for) such failures in Judaeo-Christian religion or other contemporary major world religions. He would not have had to look very far: "Hath the rain a father" (the phrase he cites to illustrate the spirit of scientific curiosity in the Bible) implies an assumption of personal, anthropomorphic agency for a natural process, the very error of thought for which Meteora's minions are dismissed.

At its best, the dichotomy of myth and religion that, without explication, pervades Capra's films is a contrast between less and more subtle metaphysical concepts; at its worst, it smacks of the view that Capra's religion, along with other recognized world religions, make up religion, while distant—that is, archaic, dead, or "exotic"—religions make up mythology. As noted, James Gilbert (1997) offers an admirable analysis of the strategies of interrelating science and religion in the films discussed here, discussing some of the examples just mentioned. He focuses especially on the complex, behind-the-scenes negotiations about the relation of science and religion that went on among writers, ad agency, science advisers, and other parties responsible for the films. But I cannot help but notice the almost total absence of commentary in his analysis of the third concept, mythology, and the crucial role it plays—one so well established that it now goes by without notice: that of "taking the fall" for the failures of religion in portraying the physical cosmos. Religion in effect comes to mean all that is noble in religion, mythology all that is inadequate in it. Mythology is both failed science *and* failed religion. Mythology and science diverge precisely so religion and science can converge. Yet mythology survives in Capra's cosmos, finding its place as artistic fiction. Of mythology, religion, and science, it is with the first that Capra's career has the most affinities. He is not the researcher of science or the priest or prophet of religion; but as a creator of artistic fictions he promotes the harmonizing of the two great spheres of nonfictional human existence: science and religion. Mythology survives as Capra.

A contrast between realistic photography and studio animation is used to portray religion, science, and myth through an underlying rule of distribution that admits few exceptions: religion is portrayed though realistic photographs (of symbols, rituals, shrines, for example), while myth is portrayed through cartoon animation. The scientific explanation of nature is portrayed through a process of juxtaposition in which the animateds are dismissed (or reduced in the sense noted earlier), while realistic photography emerges as the index of the real, common to science and religion.[10]

***

It would be difficult to establish just how much of the view offered in these films is unedited Capra. In his autobiography, Capra is upbeat: the president of AT&T (Bell Telephone's parent company) wanted Capra as someone "expert in science and entertainment" and told him that "after you there is no second choice" (Capra 1997:440). It was a joyous enterprise for Capra, who describes himself while working on these films as "living in the sensuous fires of enthusiasm" (ibid.:443) and exercising autonomy and control over the project. Capra cites the positive reviews and lingers especially on expressions of appreciation he received from ordinary people.

Most interesting, Capra's account of the origins of the project contains a scenario reminiscent of the formula of the films themselves; it unfolds as Capra sits at a table with the president of AT&T and the members of that company's Scientific Advisory Committee—"a collection of minds that had to be among the most brilliant in the nation" (ibid.:440). The scenario Capra presents is this select group of scientists convincing Capra to do the science films after he had decided he wanted out: "Finally Dean Harrison, the physicist from M.I.T., spoke up. 'Frank Capra, scientists feel there is a gulf, a widening gulf between science on one side and Mr. Average Citizen on the other. We have become members of this Advisory Committee in the hope that we can help you build a bridge across this gulf . . . You build such a bridge, Frank Capra, and you will accomplish much for yourself and the Telephone Company, but much more for the nation and perhaps for the world'" (ibid.:442).

Capra called attention to his religious convictions, including the fact that he was "Catholic in *spirit*," a "*wacky* Catholic," with the expectation that this would raise concerns among the scientists: "'Gentlemen, I'm not your man,' I said to the Committee scientists in the privacy of a Board room. 'You gentlemen are scientists. A physical fact is your truth, your bible, your discipline. Well, to me a physical fact is boring, unless—it is illuminated by a touch of the Eternal. So you see, if I make a science film I will have to say that scientific research is just another expression of the Holy Spirit that works in *all* men.'" (ibid.)

The science advisers' reaction to this and other potential difficulties he raised was, according to Capra, a dismissive "so?"

Capra at the meeting is Hemo or Mr. Sun, fearful that science wants a picture of the universe built out of only stark, cold facts. The science advisers at the meeting play the role played by Dr. Research in the films, convincing the fearful (Capra in this case) that science does not require the jettisoning of a spiritual dimension. In his biography of Capra, Joseph McBride (2000:77) points out that the motif of glimpsing the eternal occurs in Capra's *Lost Horizon* and *State of the Union*. Finally, a glimpse of the eternal also seems to me a fitting description of the look Capra is going for in the tableaux of wonder scenes I discussed earlier; he wants to present science as an avenue to such a glimpse.

Capra summarizes his achievement in these films: "By weaving together live scenes, fantasy, traceries of diagrams, animated cartoon characters, puppets, and—above all—humorous illustrative parables, metaphors, similes, and analogies, we reduced the complex to the simple, the eternal to the everyday . . . I built a small bridge that spanned the gulf twixt scientific and commoner. Spanned it by making education as exciting and entertaining as any comedy, drama, or whodunit" (Capra 1997:443).

Others paint a more complex picture. The record of the negotiations behind the films presented by Gilbert (1997:199–223) suggests that Capra faced considerable resistance regarding the infusion of religious sentiments into them. McBride (2000:612) says that AT&T was trying to "boost its corporate image and to brighten the benighted postwar image of science" and that Capra suffered from guilt from having been a secret informer during the McCarthy era and saw the science project as "rehabilitating his own image" (ibid.:613). Having done war propaganda, the science films marked "a return to propaganda, although of the more sophisticated Madison Avenue variety" (ibid.:612).

But amid a complex web of motives and feelings, Capra does seem to have maintained a consistent and genuine enthusiasm for science. His early studies at Caltech appear to have set in motion a lifelong fascination. Befitting the phrase "the catastrophe of success" from his title, McBride chooses to end his biography with a conversation in which Capra expresses regret in having forsaken his scientific ambitions for film (ibid.:654–55).

Among other things, Capra tells him that he would have ended up as an astronomer: "I could study the stars and the planets forever. I always wanted to know why, *why*" (ibid.655).

The chance to make films about this enthusiasm and directed to an audience with children in the front rows also afforded an opportunity to extend the life of the optimistic formula that, having propelled Capra's career during the Depression years, by the postwar period had grown tired. This now-aging formula was deployed within an even older framework for assigning science and its neighbors, mythology and religion, their rightful respective places in history and in human life, a framework given shape in the eighteenth-century philosophers of the Enlightenment and now dis-seminated through popular science and mass entertainment. If science cre-ates the future, science popularizing often works by fitting this future into successful formulas of the past.

POSTSCRIPT

Since completing this chapter, I had the good fortune to interview the big three—Mr. Sun, Hemo, and Meteora—at a get-together held to talk about a possible jubilee, encouraged in part by the recent wave of nostalgic interest in them and by the many related film clips on the Web. I was particularly interested in finding out their thoughts about how the films would play now in terms of "political correctness." An excerpt of the interview can be found by going to http://www.indiana.edu/~folklore/inprogress.shtml and follow-ing the link to the Interview with Hemo and the Gang.

NOTES

1. The term is obviously less graceful than animé, but the latter is now strongly associ-ated with specifically Japanese animation.

2. In "real life," Dr. Research was Frank Baxter, a professor of literature and a television personality.

3. See the letter of Frank P. Keller in Scherle and Levy (1977:253).

4. McBride (2000:46) says that Capra regarded his parents as "ignorant and supersti-tious peasants"; in a scenario common in immigrant families, his education opened a painful rift between him and them. Might at some level that social rift inform the portrayal of the cartoon yokels who are slow, suspicious of outsiders, and predisposed to close ranks against the new?

5. A snippet from the "Ode to Joy" from Beethoven's Ninth Symphony also appears in the closing background music from Capra's *Meet John Doe*.

6. Among the best sources on Enlightenment views of mythology are Feldman and Rich-ardson (1975) and Manuel (1959).

7. The view of Tylor summarized here is indebted to the research of George Stocking (see especially 1968); I discuss Tylor's epistemology in Schrempp (1983).

8. The AI strategy of "homuncular functionalism" proceeds by breaking a brain down into constituent functions—for example, "executive," "librarian," "facilitator"—metaphorically termed "homunculi." Dr. Research's animated little men thus amount to a sort of cartoon literalization (if such is possible) of a serious science metaphor (see Schrempp 2012: chapter 5).

9. Hope figures as a major theme in many of Capra's films, most explicitly perhaps in *Meet John Doe*.

10. The juxtaposition of animated cartoons and photographic realism breaks down into a more finely graded continuum. Between these lie a variety of intermediate forms, including a cartoon green creature representing chlorophyll in photosynthesis and several cartoon professors (ultimately, is there any other kind?), Professor Coriolis and Professor Anatomy, representing their respective branches of scientific research.

7

Departures from Earth I
The Ferris Wheel and the Deep-Space Probe

And I, if I be lifted up from the earth, will draw all things to myself.

(John 12:32)

"Epiphany," "peak experience," "the sublime," "flow," "aha moment": these are some of the many terms—bearing a family resemblance while differing in tone and connotation—through which analytical thinkers have sought to identify and characterize moments of intense, transcendent, harmonizing personal experience. The converse is also possible: equally intense, personal glimpses of cosmic disharmony and disconnection. Because we tend to equate literary writing with storytelling, it is important to take cognizance of this exception: some of the most intense literary moments inhere not in narrative but in literarily conveyed cosmic visions—though, of course, these visions sometimes emerge as pauses in a narrative flow. My purpose in this chapter is to explore examples of visionary cosmic moments from popular science writing, with parallel moments taken from literature outside the exposition of science, in order to allow such writings to cast light on both the broader literary tradition and the transformations it undergoes in the hands of popular science writers. I argue that some of the visions offered by scientists as culminating products of their craft might be seen instead as humble, "pre-scientific" moments to which a science overlay has been added.

I begin with an elementary literarily created moment of cosmic harmony—a personal favorite—from the Lake Wobegon series of monologues by Garrison Keillor (1987). I initially encountered this monologue in a radio broadcast and subsequently sought it out in published form (it occurs under the title "State Fair" in the collection of Lake Wobegon stories *Leaving*

 DOI: 10.7330/9780874219708.c007

Home [ibid.]). Keillor's observations, apparently delivered in a broadcast that originated from a state fair, are gathered around his recollections of a year in which his Aunt Myrna entered a chocolate cake in a baking contest. The account of that day at the fair concludes in a quiet, transitional tone:

> I went up in the ferris wheel for a last ride before being thrown into seventh grade. It went up into the stars and fell back to earth and rose again, and I had a magnificent vision, or think I did, though it's hard to remember if it was that year with the chocolate cake or the next one with the pigs getting loose. The ferris wheel is the same year after year. It's like all one ride to me: we go up and I think of people I knew who are dead and I smell fall in the air, manure, corn dogs, and we drop down into blazing light and blaring music. Every summer I'm a little bigger, but riding the ferris wheel, I feel the same as ever, I feel eternal. The combination of cotton candy, corn dogs, diesel smoke, and sawdust, in a hot dark summer night, it never changes, not an inch. The wheel carries us up high, high, high, and stops, and we sit swaying, creaking, in the dark, on the verge of death. You can see death from here. The wind blows from the northwest, from the farm school in Saint Anthony Park, a chilly wind with traces of pigs and sheep in it. This is my vision: little kids holding on to their daddy's hand, and he is me. He looks down on them with love and buys them another corn dog. They are worried they will lose him, they hang on to his leg with one hand, eat with the other. This vision is unbearably wonderful. Then the wheel brings me down to the ground. We get off and other people get on. Thank you, dear God, for this good life and forgive us if we do not love it enough. (ibid.:114–15)

The genre represented by this passage is by nature vulnerable, owing to its maudlin content. How different are such moments from those deep-sleep dreams in which one has a sense of world-altering profundity that one cannot recall on waking (or, to the extent that one can recall them, cannot find in them anything profound)—for that matter, from the sense of the oneness of all being that comes with inebriation. Aesthetically, however, there is something noble in the idea of being led to that state by mere words and simple, non-technical, non-academic, non-sophisticated ones at that.

The simplicity of Keillor's scenario—an account of a sort of folk-religious ecstasy, seemingly open to anyone with access to a Ferris wheel—is belied by the subtlety of the written text, for an analysis reveals that the effect of the passage has been carefully prepared by the entire monologue, the specifics of the baking contest appearing almost as a diversion that allows for a surreptitious setting up of the cosmic amid the comic. Either Keillor's mind effortlessly marshals cosmic symbols, or else he is adept in making the laborious appear spontaneous. The cosmic moment genre indeed may have a very small window in which it can succeed. In my experience of Keillor's passage, the written version was vastly less intense in effect than the spoken one, and the reader of my analysis will be at yet another degree of removal. I can only attest that, as I listened, there was a momentary coalescence of the author's speaking voice and the hearer's mood that produced a wonderful effect that, as far as I could gather from what I could hear of the reactions of Keillor's immediate audience, was not limited to me.

***

How did Keillor set up the cosmic moment? The Ferris wheel cosmic moment scene is prepared through allusions to classic religio-cosmological themes, which can be summarized in four groups.

The first is the theme of plenitude: a reveling in the variety of things in the world, both naturally occurring and of human fabrication. The assemblage of these objects is the very raison d'être of a state fair: to punctuate with spectacle—a roundup of great stuff—the routine of small-town life. There is an exuberance in spectacle that rivals the tone of many origin mythologies in litanizing the beings and regions of the cosmos. From the interstices come hints of even more mysteries; "the gypsy ticket-seller looked at me with a haughty look that said, *I know things you'll never know, what I've seen you'd never understand*" (ibid.:110). The youthfulness that allows a local, rural roundup of life to be experienced as unbounded cornucopia adds another level of emotion—that of nostalgia for lost innocence—to the cosmic ambient; like many of Keillor's reminiscences, it leaves those who remember wondering, with mixed feelings, whether this sort of experience is still available to children.

Second, right from the opening Keillor's monologue is replete with small-town inflections of the great themes of cosmic temporality: linearity and cyclicity, eternality and mortality. He announces to his audience, "I've come every year since I was five, and that's more than twenty years" (ibid.:118). Part of the annual ritual was his mother's indication that the trip would probably not occur this year:

> She said, "There's too much work to do and we can't afford it, it's too crowded, and anyway it's the same as last year. I don't see how we can do it. I'm sorry."
> It was her way of lending drama to the trip. (ibid.:109)

So, it was a yearly trip to a yearly event, set at harvest time to mark the culmination and beginning of the end of the farmers' year, or canning season as it is known in the rural vernacular. The Ferris wheel is a microcosm, a wheel within a wheel, a revolution within the larger one marked by the yearly pilgrimage. Toward the end of the passage the Ferris wheel's rotation merges with the individual's life cycle, the cyclic linearity of the fair with that of human generations: the wheel stops to let some people off and others on. The language alludes to the Christian cycle of "the fall" and redemption-resurrection, as the wheel "fell back to earth and rose again." The cyclicity is punctuated with clear intrusions of linearity, most notably the reference to the beginning of seventh grade as the year in which the vision occurred (seven is a mystical number in the Judaeo-Christian cosmology, no doubt the single most important source feeding into Keillorian cosmography). But "it's hard to remember if it was that year with the chocolate cake or the next one with the pigs getting loose" (ibid.:124). Such punctuations do not lessen but rather intensify the sense of cycles by calling to attention the sameness within the difference.

Third, overlying, or perhaps pervading, the theme of plenitude, one finds, as in many other religious cosmologies, a dualism of good and evil. Religious cosmic dualism is often accompanied by the notion that the opposed qualities are transcendable and possibly mysteriously balanced and interrelated, a pattern Carl Gustav Jung studied as *coniuntio oppositorum,* or "union of opposites."[1] Keillor recalls:

> Because we were Christians we gave a wide berth to the Midway, where ladies danced and did other things at the Persian Palms and Harlem Revue tent shows. We avoided sin, but it was exciting for me to be so close to it . . .
> I loved the Fair, the good and the bad. (ibid.:110)

The stark moral dualism continues to be elaborated through a number of side-references, including those to foods; for instance, Keillor and his relatives had devised the term *chocolate angel food* cake so as not to encourage Satan. Musing on angels visiting the Earth, Keillor suspects that corndogs would not be their food (ibid.:112). The religious puritanism that shaped his community and his memories of growing up figures strongly in Keillor's monologues of reminiscence. But mixed in with this theme, less directly in this monologue than in others yet always in the background, is his intense experience of small-town readiness to vilify desires that cannot be satisfied by small-town life, fed by parents' fears of losing children to those desires. Resentment toward such small-town parochialism—the dark side of the hand-holding between generations seen from the Ferris wheel (discussed earlier)—seems to be one of Keillor's creative demons.

***

Fourth, the idea of a preternaturally distanced vantage that allows the integration of the cosmic totality operates powerfully in Judaeo-Christian cosmology; in the context of science it reappears as a metaphor of scientific objectivity (i.e., the "god's-eye view"). A number of scriptural passages allude to the integrative view occasioned by distance, whether in the concrete form of a Creator envisioning a cosmos from without, the ascent of a holy mountain, or the more enigmatic biblical passage cited as an epigram above ("if I be lifted up"). The latter passage has occasioned considerable debate, but lost in the search for cryptic meaning is the most basic fact of perception: that mere distancing results in the broadening of one's physical field of view.

Popular science writers also employ the cosmic moment genre. I would like to compare Garrison Keillor's "State Fair" cosmic moment with one offered by Carl Sagan (1994) in *Pale Blue Dot*.[2] Sagan's moment, like Keillor's, is triggered by an atypically distanced view of things, though in this case the distance in absolute terms is considerably greater. Specifically, as part of an attempt to offer a glitzy visualization of the Copernican lesson—the lesson that we must give up the view of our central, special place in the cosmos— Sagan recounts how he and others convinced a cash-strapped NASA of the post-Apollo era to instruct the *Voyager* deep-space probe to photograph the Earth, and the sun's other planets, as it passed beyond the edge of the solar system.[3] From this vantage, the Earth should have appeared as an insignificant entity, much like other planets and stars appear from Earth. By a quirk, the Earth in its photograph (and alone of all the planets) appeared to sit in a shaft of light, eerily reminiscent of the beams of heavenly light found in many religious greeting cards. Sagan was forced to explain: "Because of the reflection of sunlight off the spacecraft, the Earth seems to be sitting in a beam of light, as if there were some special significance to this small world. But it's just an accident of geometry and optics. The Sun emits its radiation equitably in all directions. Had the picture been taken a little earlier or a little later, there would have been no sunbeam highlighting the Earth" (ibid.:8).

Interestingly, however, a few paragraphs later Sagan takes advantage of the illusion to attempt a cosmic moment:

> Look again at that dot. That's here. That's home. That's us. On it everyone you love, everyone you know, everyone you ever heard of, every human being who ever was, lived out their lives. The aggregate of our joy and suffering, thousands of confident religions, ideologies and economic

doctrines, every hunter and forager, every hero and coward, every creator
and destroyer of civilization, every king and peasant, every young couple
in love, every mother and father, hopeful child, inventor and explorer,
every teacher of morals, every corrupt politician, every "superstar," every
"supreme leader," every saint and sinner in the history of our species lived
there—on a mote of dust suspended in a sunbeam. (ibid.:8)

The mote of dust in the sunbeam, in this oft-quoted passage, offers a
sort of secular alternative to the theme of a heavenly guiding beacon that a
religiously inclined commentator might have gotten out of the photographic
quirk. Note the similarities to the humbler version of Keillor. Keillor says
he loves it all, the good and the bad; while Sagan's litany contains saints and
sinners, creators and destroyers.

Verbose and obviously inferior *literarily* to Keillor's cosmic moment,
Sagan's is nonetheless created from the same ingredients: distanced vision,
plentitude, dualism, and themes of cosmic temporality. Sagan utilizes
something like a litany to create an aura of plenitude for the small dot
(which is situated between "billions 'n billions" of celestial bodies); and
many of the elements of the litany juxtapose polar terms, suggesting a
moral duality, if not union of opposites. Finally, Sagan makes deep and
repeated use of cosmic themes of linearity and cyclicity; these occur in
allusions to life cycles and generations within the key passage itself but
even more so in the lead-up and larger argument of his book, which is a
plea that we should support exploration and colonization of the universe.
The opening line of the introduction is "We were wanderers from the
beginning" (ibid.:xi). Sagan goes on to depict various rounds of human
explorations, from hunter-gatherer nomadism to great prehistoric and historic migrations and seafaring explorations. Space exploration marks the
next logical round of exploration. As noted, one part of Keillor's vision is
children hanging onto their parents, afraid of losing them; his vision, in
other words, unifies not just spatio-synoptically but also temporally and
intergenerationally. Paralleling Keillor but on a grander scale, Sagan moves
through personal history with stories about his American-immigrant
ancestors. Beyond these, in the final chapter, Sagan's closing paean to the
spirit of exploration begins in the pre-human evolutionary world: "Fish
with rudimentary lungs and fins slightly adapted for walking must have
died in great numbers before establishing a permanent foothold on land"
(ibid.:403). Continuing the great drama, space exploration thus not only
binds the cosmos through diaspora but "binds the generations" of human
and pre-human life (ibid.:405). All of this is set out amid orbital cycles of
various magnitudes.

Finally, consider what is not actually visible in the photograph from *Voyager*. Except for the "sunbeam" supplied by accidental lens flare, the Earth appears as a tiny light dot against a dark background—and I do not dispute that the photograph provides a thought-provoking view of our planet. But not even the Earth's grossest geographic features are visible in the photograph, let alone any saints or sinners. In hearing or reading Keillor's "State Fair" vision, one can realistically imagine rising on a Ferris wheel to actually see, hear, smell the entire cosmos—kids, dads, sheep, corndogs, and all—but not so in Sagan's: the contents of Sagan's pale blue dot litany come entirely from his head (and ours). The situation is interestingly ironic. For throughout Sagan's writing, and nowhere more so than in his essay "The Man in the Moon and the Face on Mars" (ibid.:41–59), runs a warning that we should resist projecting anthropocentric images onto the distant entities of the cosmos; yet here he is inviting us to do just that. The instance in which the Earth itself is the distant cosmic entity would seem to constitute the one exception. We are asked to overlay the high-tech, objective, distanced photographic documentation of Earth with our everyday anthropocentric experience. But, as suggested by the comparison with Keillor, the latter is the constant of the vision, the former the variable: if you haven't got a deep-space probe, a Ferris wheel will do.

Much popular science writing deals with cosmology, and such cosmic moments are one part of the fare offered to the reader; yet there is nothing intrinsically scientific about the genre of cosmic moments. The specific contents comprised in cosmic moments are highly variable and can stem as easily from quotidian experience as from scientific investigation; moreover, the same visionary statement might be taken as inflecting either a religious-mystical or a scientific sensibility. Richard Dawkins says as much, citing the famous stanza from William Blake's "Auguries of Innocence" about the "world in a grain of sand." Noting that he wished that he himself had written the lines, Dawkins comments: "The stanza can be read as all about science, all about standing in the moving spotlight, about taming space and time, about the very large built from the quantum graininess of the very small, a lone flower as a miniature of all evolution. The impulses to awe, reverence and wonder which led Blake to mysticism (and lesser figures to paranormal superstition . . .) are precisely those that lead others of us to science. Our interpretation is different but what excites us is the same" (Dawkins 1998:17).

As noted, the experience of viewing our everyday Earth from a non-quotidian distance seems to be one possible triggering mechanism, and certainly it is a framing device, for such cosmic moments. But the experience of a shift—a jolt reminding us that our field of view is not necessarily coterminous with the cosmos—is more important than the absolute distance that triggers the shift. Moreover, even the stupendous feats of science in imaging technology (microscopic, telescopic, various types and methods of visual enhancement) do not automatically translate into aesthetic excellence or moral power of cosmic vision. In terms of several factors, including the distance and technology involved and the authorial voice tapped, Sagan and Keillor mark opposite ends of a continuum. Sagan claims (humanly speaking) enormous distance, advanced technology, and abstract science; Keillor claims small-town distance, low technology, and the voice of basic humanity.[4] Interestingly, the scalar differences that fundamentally distinguish Sagan's observational frame from Keillor's are creatively and conveniently suspended by both writers, in ways that bring the two visions closer to one another. Keillor says the Ferris wheel took him "up into the stars"—at least a minor exaggeration—while Sagan, in portraying the Earth as "suspended" in a sunbeam, suspends something else: the scientific fact that on a cosmic scale the up-and-down direction, implied by "suspended," has no meaning. As though to balance the poetic liberty taken for the sake of the vision, the same photograph also appears on the reverse side of Sagan's title page, this time with the "sunbeam" positioned transversely rather than vertically, with the caption "The Earth: a pale blue dot in a sunbeam"; from a scientific-point perspective, neither the vertical nor horizontal orientation of the image is more correct.

Harmonious cosmic moments stem not so much from religion, literature, or science but from a capacity that, for whatever reason, is part of our mind's equipment and which religion, literature, and science appropriate to their respective means and ends.

***

A particularly intriguing and earnest cosmic moment, one often revisited, occurs as the closing of Steven Weinberg's classic *The First Three Minutes*, a popular explanation of the "big bang" theory:

> It is almost irresistable for humans to believe that we have some special relation to the universe . . . As I write this I happen to be in an airplane at 30,000 feet, flying over Wyoming en route home from San Francisco to Boston. Below, the earth looks very soft and comfortable—fluffy clouds here and there, snow turning pink as the sun sets, roads stretching straight across the country from one town to another. It is very hard to realize that this all is just a tiny part of an overwhelmingly hostile universe. It is even harder to realize that this present universe has evolved from an unspeakably unfamiliar early condition, and faces a future extinction of endless cold or

intolerable heat. The more the universe seems comprehensible, the more it also seems pointless.

But if there is no solace in the fruits of our research, there is at least some consolation in the research itself. Men and women are not content to comfort themselves with tales of gods and giants, or to confine their thoughts to the daily affairs of life; they also build telescopes and satellites and accelerators, and sit at their desks for endless hours working out the meaning of the data they gather. The effort to understand the universe is one of the very few things that lifts human life a little above the level of farce, and gives it some of the grace of tragedy. (Weinberg 1984:143–44)[5]

We encounter once again in Weinberg's vision the same basic ingredients outlined earlier (except perhaps plenitude, although there is surely at least a hint of this in the topic of Weinberg's book—the origin of the cosmos). Weinberg's closing rumination is immediately preceded and prompted by debates on the temporal character of the physical cosmos, specifically the debates among scientific cosmologists about whether the universe will keep expanding, collapse, or oscillate in endless cycles (ibid.:143). Interestingly, after a treatise involving astronomical distances, it is rather a perspective only slightly distanced, cosmologically speaking—a view of the earth from an airplane—that prompts Weinberg's musings. Most intriguing, however, is the moral polarity between the seeming hospitality of the earth and the hostility of cosmos at large: the long (cosmic) distance leaves him cold, the short (airplane) distance leaves him warm. Even though these musings lack the exuberance of Keillor's and Sagan's visions—indeed, through a principled refusal to be seduced by fluffy clouds into cosmic sentimentality, they express a cosmic disharmony—Weinberg in the end arrives at a humanly compelling, mediating concept in the idea of tragedy, which since Aristotle has been thought of as a confluence of moral opposites: the doings of (at least partially) good people caught in bad circumstances.

As a mythologist, I also cannot help but note one other union of opposites that occurs in the final pages of Weinberg's book (immediately preceding the passage quoted above). Specifically, Weinberg opens *The First Three Minutes* by setting up mythology as a foil, or nemesis, of science. He summarizes an origin story from Norse mythology and argues that it presents an unsatisfying view of the cosmos that science can remedy. But as he draws his book to a close, Weinberg discusses scientific scenarios of the possible end of the universe, and here he draws from the same Norse mythological tradition—specifically, the eschatological story of Ragnarök. This time Weinberg presents the mythological story not in opposition to, but rather as dovetailing with, one of the possible scenarios recognized by science (ibid.).

***

Notes of tragedy are not confined to those cosmic moments that belong to science. Here, the famous concluding vision of Norman Maclean's *A River Runs through It* is instructive:

> Now nearly all those I loved and did not understand when I was young are dead, but I still reach out to them.
>
> Of course, now I am too old to be much of a fisherman, and now of course I usually fish the big waters alone, although some friends think I shouldn't. Like many fly fishermen in western Montana where the summer days are almost Arctic in length, I often do not start fishing until the cool of the evening. Then in the Arctic half-light of the canyon, all existence fades to a being with my soul and memories and the sounds of the Big Blackfoot River and a four-count rhythm and the hope that a fish will rise.
>
> Eventually, all things merge into one, and a river runs through it. The river was cut by the world's great flood and runs over rocks from the basement of time. On some of the rocks are timeless raindrops. Under the rocks are the words, and some of the words are theirs.
>
> I am haunted by waters. (Maclean 1976:104)

Certainly, the cool of the Arctic Montana days is quite distinct from the future extinction from cold Weinberg recounts as one of the possible scenarios of the end of the universe; but these impending terminations, though of vastly different scale, are invoked by Maclean and Weinberg to roughly the same end: to conjure up a mood of contemplation regarding the meaning of human life or particular lives. Part of the power of Maclean's passage derives from the feeling it conveys of an ultimate simplification, a reduction to the essential. While the alteration of view is not, in this case, created by a physical distancing of vantage point, a change of light has much the same effect: a loss of detail that leaves only—or should we say, for the first time reveals—the broad outlines. The phrase "all things merge into one, and a river runs through it" can be taken as a literal reference to the diminishing distinctiveness of visible things as the sun sets or as a reference to the course of Maclean's life along the river or to a state of mind that emerges in the later part of the day or of life, when details give way to dominant emotional engravings—in this case, the mystery that is his brother Paul, around which Maclean's story turns. The simplification may at first seem the opposite of the theme of plenitude discussed earlier, but it is opposite only in the sense of being "the other side of the coin." Behind the increasingly dimming light looms the full set of details of a place and a life, of many intertwined lives. Beneath the fish that may rise are those that for now will remain in the depths. The river itself runs from the "basement of time," a term that, emotionally speaking, would seem to be a rough equivalent of "the first three minutes."

***

Several other commonalities should be noted. The terminal stage, or at least the ending of one cycle in anticipation of the new, is the temporal location of all the cosmic moments considered above (Keillor's final circuit in the Ferris wheel for that year; for Sagan, the space probe *Voyager*'s last glimpse of Earth as it leaves the solar system, taking with it, for the moment, the American space program; Weinberg's reflections on the end of the physical cosmos, balancing his exposition of the first three minutes; Maclean's late-in-life comments in the declining daylight). A particularly dramatic version of the finality of the cosmic moment occurs in Ambrose Bierce's "Occurrence at Owl Creek Bridge," perhaps best known from a film that was made from the story. Bierce combines the theme of being lifted up with emergence from the depths of water: the main character is a captured soldier being hanged over Owl Creek, who in his final seconds imagines the rope breaking and his plunging into the water below. Emerging, he sees life in a new way and, as if for the first time, with sharpened senses. The vision is both expansive and reductive, catching the essence of life but in its most elemental forms: veining of leaves, spider webs, blades of grass:

> Something in the awful disturbance of his organic system had so exalted and refined them that they made record of things never before perceived. He felt the ripples upon his face and heard their separate sounds as they struck. He looked at the forest on the bank of the stream, saw the individual trees, the leaves and the veining of each leaf—saw the very insects upon them: the locusts, the brilliant flies, the gray spiders stretching their webs from twig to twig. He noted the prismatic colors in all the dewdrops upon a million blades of grass. (Bierce 1946:14)

Despite the possibility of the ritualization of such experiences, they are usually portrayed as spontaneous, coincidental, unanticipated in their occurrence. This is especially noticeable in the scientists' accounts: the photographic quirk that bequeaths to Sagan the image of a dust mote in a sunbeam; the fact that Weinberg happens to be looking down from an airplane on an inviting, warm earth as he ponders the end of the universe and the conclusion of his book.

The temporal concepts of cosmic moments are accompanied by spatial conceits. Traditional cosmogonic myths in general favor the vertical over the horizontal as the dimension in which the cosmos first opens up: sky and earth are separated or propped apart, humans are born from below the earth's surface, land is first fished up out of the sea depths, and the waters above the firmament are separated from those below before sea and land are separated. We can only speculate about the reasons for this inclination—perhaps that a cosmic *effort* is most readily portrayed against the tendency toward universal collapse inherent in the law of gravity or, less loftily, that the daily challenge of "getting up" precedes that of "going out." Whatever the reason, the literary cosmic visions mentioned here all share in the privileging of the vertical. Keillor is lifted up by, and looks down from, a Ferris wheel. In Maclean's final paragraph, the river running "through" is suddenly surrounded by references to above and below: "the hope that a fish will rise," the river being "cut" into earth and running over rocks from "the basement of time," and words lying "under the rocks." Bierce's final scene is constructed around a "hanging" that gives way to a plunge into the watery depths and, from there, a vision aimed upward. As noted, Weinberg looks down from the airplane, and Sagan chooses (in the face of cosmic arbitrariness) to orient the *Voyager* "sunbeam" vertically; both fall right in line with the literary and mythological privileging of the vertical over the horizontal in the conjuring of cosmic moments. One of Weinberg's (2003) later books is titled *Facing Up*, and the book's cover bears the image of astronomer Tycho Brahe looking upward, transfixed, at the sky; Weinberg juxtaposes this facing up to the need to psychologically face up to the reality of an impersonal cosmos.

Finally, in these visions, whether literary or scientific, the large serves the small. The cosmic moment genre takes as its charge, its raison d'être, to proclaim the inadequacy of everyday understandings of the world, even though that which is imparted in such breakthrough moments might be a mere *intensification* of a message ultimately maudlin; what is remedied is not our vision of the whole but, *through the whole*, our vision of the local human situation within. After rehearsing the usual direction of science—to push further—Sagan and Weinberg return to the earth to impart new visions of human life on it. The two literary figures, Keillor and Maclean, are moved by failures in humans' attempts to understand human life in its ordinary sense, especially our attempts to understand one another. Maclean's account of his own, and more especially his father's, ongoing anguish at their failure to understand their brother/son Paul haunts the entire story and builds to the final vision.

Within Keillor's vision we encounter regret at failure to love life enough, but this transcendent vision itself is immediately preceded by a humble— and very funny, in the spoken version at least—lesson in human misunderstanding. After a day of suffering in silence from having to wear a rayon shirt to the fair, he says to his mother, " 'This is the last time I wear a rayon shirt, I hate them.' She said, 'All right, that's fine.' I said, 'You're not mad?' She said, 'No, I thought you liked them, that's all' " (Keillor 1987:114). Misunderstanding is the immediate precursor and precipitator of heightened understanding; it is just after narrating this incident that Keillor launches into his small-town, Ferris wheel cosmic vision. Likewise, it is just after explaining the technical distortion cause by lens flare that Sagan, inverting his original intent, redeploys the photographic "miscommunication" from the edge of the solar system as a cosmo-humanistic vision.

NOTES

1. On "union of opposites," see El-Shamy and Schrempp (2005).

2. Elsewhere (Schrempp 2012a: chapter 6) I offer a fuller discussion of Sagan's vision as elaborated within the framework of *Pale Blue Dot*. My purpose in the present chapter goes in the opposite direction, removing Sagan's vision from his own book and comparing it with visions announced by other writers from very different intellectual traditions.

3. The *Voyager* photographs of the planets, grouped together as a "family portrait" (more technically, NASA image PIA00453), can be found on several websites (for example, http://photojournal.jpl.nasa.gov/catalog/PIA00453, accessed July 6, 2014). On August 27, 2013, an intriguing NPR news story discussed a new photo of Earth from the distance, this time taken by a probe near Saturn. The commentator related the new photo to the one that inspired Sagan's now-classic vision and played a recording of Sagan reading the famous "suspended in a sunbeam" passage (the story—"NASA Uses Photo of Earth from Saturn to Boost Space Interest"—and recording can be heard at http://www.npr.org/player/v2/mediaPlayer.html?action=1&t=1&islist=false&id=204895903&m=204895908, accessed July 6, 2014). Another tribute to the passage occurs in a recent article about Sagan in *Smithsonian* magazine (Achenbach 2014:71). Achenbach, commenting on the spoken version of the passage, describes Sagan as "filling the auditorium with his baritone, lingering luxuriantly on his consonants as always" (ibid.).

4. Keillor's Mark Twain–like anecdotal reminiscences, to which "State Fair" belongs, are backed in his radio broadcasts by several other comedic variants of the voice of basic humanity—including cowboys, in "The Lives of the Cowboys" sketches, and detective novels, in the "Guy Noir" sets. Variants of the detective novel genre tapped within other genres are also considered in chapter 8, on cosmic disharmony, and chapter 9, in an analysis of Tom Stoppard's play *Jumpers*.

5. Among the many responses to Weinberg's comment are Horgan (1997:73) and Davies (2007:16) and a more literarily shaped appraisal by Updike (2000:578–86).

8

Departures from Earth II
The Reason(s) for the Tragedy of Space Shuttle Columbia

THE "COSMIC MOMENTS" CONSIDERED IN CHAPTER 7 WERE built around feelings of interconnections between ourselves and the cosmos. Weinberg marked an exception in his insistence on a cosmos hostile to us; yet even he finds a meaningful, if tragic, cosmic purpose in our scientific enterprise of attempting to understand the cosmos. Intense aesthetic and moral experiences are to be had in such moments. However, another kind of intense experience is found in the opposite direction: in dramatizing the fault lines of the cosmos and elaborating its main constituents agonistically rather than integratively; Weinberg's comment starts us in that direction.

William Langewiesche's "Columbia's Last Flight: The Inside Story of the Investigation—and the Catastrophe It Laid Bare" (Langewiesche 2003) is a detailed investigative article that presents the science and technology of the disaster that befell the space shuttle *Columbia*, along with the "human" factors that figured in the tragedy. Langewiesche is a high-profile, award-winning writer with a penchant for analyzing disasters and their lessons (from airliner crashes to the World Trade Center, the modern skyscraper marking another form of departure from earth). Currently, he is international correspondent at *Vanity Fair* magazine; before that he was national correspondent for *Atlantic Monthly* magazine.

The shuttle disaster (the second of two disasters involving space shuttles) is of recent memory: *Columbia* broke up over Texas in February 2003 as it descended from orbit and headed toward a planned landing at the Kennedy Space Center in Florida. All seven astronauts perished, and debris from the shuttle lay strewn over a 300-mile path in Texas and Louisiana. A commission of investigation after seven months concluded, against considerable initial resistance to the idea, that the proximate physical cause was foam insulation breaking off the external fuel tank during takeoff, ripping

DOI: 10.7330/9780874219708.c008

a hole in the left wing. During the subsequent reentry, hot gasses were able to penetrate inside the wing and melt structural members, leading to the breakup of the craft.

Langewiesche's (ibid.) article provides gripping reading, thanks in no small part to the deft treatment of the scientific-technological dimension of the disaster even amid its human pathos. The article is a rich site for exploring ways popular writers can make science compelling and expound on its place in human existence. Clearly, the factors that make Langewiesche a compelling writer can be described in many ways and at many levels. He employs a number of effective strategies, including a sophisticated temporalizing that includes multilevel flashbacks and flash-forwards as well as shifts in tempo. He is a pilot, and one wonders whether this gives him an advantage with such topics since, despite the wonders of engineering, a life in the air remains—now as for Icarus—a glaring form of hubris, a refusal to accept the most basic limit that nature has allotted our species. Who better than a pilot to have a feel for such things?

However, for present purposes I will prescind from all factors of Langewiesche's writing save the big issue alluded to above. Specifically, I argue that much of the deep drama of Langewiesche's piece—much of what makes it gripping—stems from an underlying separation of his discourse into three discourses, each ultimately inspired by a distinct category of stuff in the cosmos, each category signaled by and demanding a distinct way of talking. The drama, in other words, derives first and foremost from an underlying agonistic rendition of the relationships among these three different spheres in which humans exist; in addition, numerous skillful transitions and transgressions test and ultimately vindicate and amplify the lines between them.

Briefly, the three spheres that underlie Langewiesche's (ibid.) analysis— the ontologically incommensurable entities of the cosmos—are *inanimate matter*, society in the form of *bureaucracy*, and unique *human personalities*. Langewiesche responds to each of these spheres with a literary genre appropriate to it, offering a full account that juxtaposes and alternately highlights each. His scientific-technological discussions read much like many other contemporary works in the genre of popular science writing; the overriding goal is to find friendly and clever ways to explain complex, technical matters to non-specialist readers. His discussion of bureaucracy, by contrast, reflects a blending of sociological sensibility and journalistic style—a combination given momentum in the crisis over the global "competitiveness" of corporations that developed during the 1980s. This perspective is signaled nowadays by application of the term *culture* to specific institutions; at issue here is the culture of NASA. Finally, Langewiesche attempts to add a dimension of "human interest" through moments in which the character and actions of particular individuals are broached in brief novelistic interludes.

This analysis focuses on one recent detailed article in the *Atlantic Monthly*, but variations on this multi-generic changeup strategy are rather common in contemporary middle-brow magazines. There are good philosophical reasons for, and indeed a long tradition behind, such distinctions; in varying ways, the spheres that Langewiesche (ibid.) distinguishes recall, for example, Aristotle's four causes, eighteenth-century philosopher Auguste Comte's hierarchy of laws operating in the cosmos (each of which motivated a particular academic discipline), and twentieth-century social scientists Talcott Parsons and Edward Shils's (1951) classic attempt to schematize multiple levels of analysis implicated in any human action.[1] Most intriguing, the three spheres align with three great divisions often recognized in the cosmic totality and, correspondingly, in the organization of academia: the inanimate (matter), the organic (bureaucracy), and the mental (individual personalities). The alignment suggested here between the organic and bureaucracy is only slightly strained. Bureaucracies meld together many human minds, but the super-organism that emerges in Langewiesche's portrayal resembles nothing so much as an amoeba: life in its most unthinking, reactive, self-protective, self-propagating mode. But the spheres can be effectively drawn into the service of entertainment, whether low grade or high; the incommensurability between them underpins countless dramatic conflicts and literary plots. Langewiesche informs us about three categories of stuff that are largely foreign to one another and perennially at war.

***

The first of the spheres, inanimate matter, calls forth the aura and some of the more obvious conventions of scientific discourse, including a quantitative emphasis, a mood of dispassionate distance (Langewiesche [2003:73] at one point uses the term *engineering cool*), and a smattering of technical terminology and jargon. Now, many thinkers, in hopes of creating a scientific sociology or psychology, cultivate these same discourse characteristics in analyses of bureaucracies and human individuals; but not Langewiesche, who reserves the scientific way of talking mainly for describing the realities of inanimate matter. To be sure, most of the scientific discourse in Langewiesche revolves around inanimate matter that has been shaped into human artifacts, notably the shuttle itself as a machine. But inanimate matter is no less subject to the laws of nature for having been engineered. The description of the normal reentry runs:

Ultimately the shuttle must return to Earth and land. The problem then is what to do with the vast amount of physical energy that has been invested in it—almost all the calories once contained in the nearly four million pounds of rocket fuel that was used to shove the shuttle into orbit. Some of that energy now resides in the vehicle's altitude, but most resides in its speed. The re-entry is a descent to a landing, yes, but primarily it is a giant deceleration, during which atmospheric resistance is used to convert velocity into heat, and to slow the shuttle by roughly 17,000 mph, so that it finally passes overhead the runway in Florida at airline speeds, and circles down to touch the ground at a well tamed 224 mph or less. Once the shuttle is on the runway, the drag chute and brakes take care of the rest. (ibid.:71)

In this passage we encounter terms familiar in human social and economic life ("invested," "calories," "resides," "tamed"), but they are subsumed into an otherwise dispassionate rendition of the physics of leaving Earth's orbit—as if to drive home the lesson that, in space flight, domesticity yields to physics. The sense of responsibility to be objective, felt in the passage, is heightened by its placement. For Langewiesche immediately precedes this account of the physics of reentry with an intensely subjective account (implicating "you") of the Earth seen from orbit, based on a specific astronaut's rendition. Its enthusiasm is suggested in this excerpt: "You come to Chicago and its lakefront, from which point you can see past Detroit and Cleveland all the way to New York. These are big cities, you think. And because you grew up on a farm in Michigan . . ." (ibid.:71). Langewiesche overlays the transition from orbit to reentry with transitions in focus and style: from novelistic to scientific, from subjective to objective, from man to machine.

In the earlier description of the engineering challenges of reentry and other similarly wrought passages throughout the article, quantitative factors are emphasized, sometimes to a degree of precision surely intended for "effect." (What other than effect is the average reader to gain from the knowledge that the shuttle has 24,305 tiles?) Such passages are also peppered with examples and brief explanations of technical terms (a wing leading-edge reinforced carbon-carbon panel is an "RCC panel"), as well as bits of flight controller talk, such as "go ahead, Macs," "four hyd return temps," and "no commonality" (ibid.:61). Some technical terms are everyday terms raised in status; instances of pieces breaking off the craft are "debris events" (ibid.:60). Once such terms are introduced, the reader must remember them to continue following the analysis.

In sum, we encounter an elaborate, otherworldly rhetoric full of compact, technical, often abbreviated but seemingly precise "cool" references that ultimately pay homage to a world of inanimate matter and its laws—a world that has been shaped and exploited by humans to their own ends and that must be understood for the investigation to proceed but which is itself finally beyond criticism or blame for the tragedy. Such rhetoric carries its own seductive power, a power enhanced by a low-key, confident delivery that succeeds in remaining friendly, as Langewiesche's does; Walter Mitty–like, we are given entrée to the world of tech-chic. Throwing in anthropomorphic tropes (e.g., the shuttle tilts nose-up to "greet the atmosphere" [ibid.:72]) in this context is a gesture of friendliness to the reader.

In many instances the world of matter, reflected in formulas of velocity, drag, and heat dissipation, bumps up against a world of human intentions and actions, which for Langewiesche demand a different sort of discourse. Striking in this regard is his terse description of a flight controller whose human instincts, perhaps amounting to nothing more than a predisposition to accept the fact that humans often arrive at their engagements a little late, overrode any physicists' abstractions about laws of motion: "Shuttles arrive on time or they don't arrive at all. But, repeatedly, the communicator radioed, '*Columbia*, Houston, UHF comm check,' as if he might still hear a reply" (ibid.:62).

One can recall a thousand artistic and philosophical works based on a pitting of humans vs. nature, either the un-engineered nature of "the elements" or the engineered nature of the "machine." Engineering engenders intensification in both of two opposite directions: who more than the engineer would face more persistently brute matter's indifference to human wishes; but, on the other hand, who more than the engineer would feel more investment of "self" in the engineered artifact?

***

Pursuing the internal diversity of Langewiesche's (ibid.) account of the *Columbia* disaster, the second type of entity the cosmos contains, besides inanimate matter, is bureaucracy; the one at issue here is NASA's. Although in limited respects lying between and blending characteristics of inanimate matter and human individuals, bureaucracy is yet, in Langewiesche's characterization, as distinct, identifiable, and sui generis as either of these other entities. Langewiesche's account gives us not the heroic dyad of man vs. the elements or an eccentric scientist building a rocket in the basement of 1950s futuristic films but rather an uneasy ménage à trois.

From Langewiesche's characterization (in which the views of chief accident investigator Hal Gehman are liberally quoted), it would seem that bureaucracies by their very nature tend toward certain defects. They are self-preserving, inbred, and prone to close ranks under perceived attack. They can suffer from inertia, fatigue, and circularity in their definition of goals. They can be rigidly hierarchical even while denying it and possibly even while unaware of it. They are subject to breakdowns in communication. Gehman is quoted: "It has been scorched into my mind that bureaucracies will do anything to defend themselves. It's not evil—it's just a natural reaction of bureaucracies, and since NASA is a bureaucracy, I expect the same out of them" (Langewiesche 2003:73).

In addition to enumerating the characteristics of bureaucracies, Langewiesche asserts a grand resemblance between the thinking and behavior of NASA's bureaucracy and that of a religious community. Central to the resemblance is the operation of non-rational doctrines and equally non-rational readiness to defend them: "The connection between the hole and the foam strike was loosely circumstantial at first, but it required serious consideration nonetheless. NASA balked at going down that road. Its reasons were not rational and scientific but, rather, complex and cultural, and they turned out to be closely related to the errors that had led to the accident in the first place: simply put, it had become a matter of faith within NASA that foam strikes—which were a known problem—could not cause mortal damage to the shuttle" (ibid.). The doctrine drew strength from each instance of a foam strike that did not cause mortal damage, and the foam became an "in-family" problem (see ibid.:78).

The third cosmic substance that played a role in the *Columbia* tragedy is an assortment of unique human personalities. In reviewing the investigation, Langewiesche says, "It was inevitable that feelings got hurt and egos squashed—and indeed that serious damage to people's lives and careers was inflicted" (ibid.:73).

The term *ego* has come to stand for the specific set of qualities that define a particular individual, as well as that individual's capacity to exert a unique causal influence in the world. Human individuals can quickly develop "gut" reactions to a situation and can also rebel against bureaucracy. The instances in which Langewiesche mentions "gut" reactions (ibid.:61, 73) involve instances in which individuals decouple from the institutional line on a particular issue. (He does not invoke "gut" in regard to anyone's feeling that things were basically okay as the *Columbia* descended, even though that appears to have been the general feeling of most controllers, at least initially.)

Several factors help explain how humans give rise to this seemingly alien thing with a life of its own: bureaucracy. Most obviously, bureaucracies are based on a submission of individual wills to formalized procedures, a hierarchical command structure, and an array of concomitants, including some factors—for example, members' persistent worry about how they will be perceived by the others—that are both necessary constituents and regrettable by-products. Without such organization and its by-products, the achievements of NASA and many other organizations would be impossible (see ibid.:69).

Interestingly, fear—specifically, individuals' fear of ridicule and fear for their careers—emerges as the salient factor that connects individual egos to bureaucracies (more on this later). Also, particular individuals are highly invested in bureaucracy. NASA administrator Sean O'Keefe is presented as a tough but non-visionary individual possessing an MA in public administration (ibid.:67). On the whole, however, in Langewiesche's presentation, the emphasis is on individuals and bureaucracies as different kinds of entities, entities at odds, if not at war, with one another—an emphasis surely related to the fact that this particular flight ended in failure and tragedy.

***

Compared with the science-aura tone toward inanimate matter and the straightforward, no-nonsense tone toward the workings of bureaucracy, Langewiesche's treatment of individuals and their roles in the disaster leans toward the novelistic—including certain gestures reminiscent of the detective novel genre. First, the investigation in fact was a detective story of sorts, a case of putting together (at one level, quite literally) the pieces of a complicated event amid allegations of coverup and resistant informants. Noting that the controllers, when they realized there had been a disaster, locked the doors and initiated "a rule-book procedure meant to stabilize and preserve the crucial last data," Langewiesche adds, "the room was being frozen as a crime scene might be" (ibid.:63).

But most intriguing is Langewiesche's characterization of several individuals who figure importantly in the unfolding tragedy. With brief introductory remarks, he attempts to put a human face on them. Especially noteworthy are four individuals. One is a shuttle pilot from whom the final radio transmission was received: "Rick Husband—Air Force test pilot, religious, good family man, always wanted to be an astronaut" (ibid.:62).

A second is the head accident investigator, Hal Gehman: "At the age of sixty, Gehman was a tall, slim, silver-haired man with an unlined face and soft eyes. Dressed in civilian clothes, standing straight but not stiffly so, he had an accessible, unassuming manner that contrasted with the rank and power he had achieved" (ibid.:63). He is profiled as competent, experienced, and ambitious but level-headed.

The third is the head of the Mission Management Team (MMT):

The once rising Linda Ham, who has come to embody NASA's arrogance and insularity in many observers' minds. Ham is the same hard-charging manager who, with a colleague, later had to be forcefully separated from the CAIB's [Columbia Accident Investigation Board] investigation. Within the strangely neutered engineering world of the Johnson Space Center, she was an intimidating figure, a youngish, attractive woman given to wearing revealing clothes, yet also known for a tough and domineering management style. Among the lower ranks she had a reputation for brooking no nonsense and being a little hard to talk to. She was not smooth. She was a woman struggling upward in a man's world. She was said to have a difficult personality. (ibid.:80)

Fourth is NASA administrator Sean O'Keefe, a "tall, balding, gray-haired man with stooped shoulders" (ibid.:84), visionless concerning space and science but schooled in budgets and management and intent on maintaining NASA's schedule. He was "an able member of Washington's revolving-door caste" (ibid.:64).

These four figures recall rather standard detective story types. There is the victim (not an enemy in the world). There is the detective-hero, whose analytical prowess is concealed by an unremarkable exterior. A subplot revolves around the fact that it was O'Keefe who invited Gehman to head the investigation, the latter surprising the former by distancing him and the rest of the NASA bureaucracy during the investigative process (see ibid.:66–67). Juxtaposed to the apparently mild-mannered detective is the ambitious woman in revealing clothes. O'Keefe is Lieutenant Tragg and Gehman is Perry Mason (of the *Perry Mason* television series); amid growing testiness, the one upholds routine procedure and decorum, the other solves the case.

The passage above is Langewiesche's only mention of sexuality and gender at NASA; clearly, it is either too much or not enough. What is the significance of Ham's alleged preference for revealing clothes? Just a few years before the *Columbia* disaster, reporters covering the affair between President Bill Clinton and Monica Lewinsky mentioned the latter's inclination to wear revealing clothes; in the case of Linda Ham, the relevance of the same detail is less clear, as there are no accompanying allegations by Langewiesche that her style caused any eyes to stray from the telemetry.[2] The inclination seems to be tapped by Langewiesche—as in detective novel strategy—as an index of ambitiousness that is distinctly female, or at least lent an extra dose of intrigue, derision, admiration, and sympathy by its unlikely source—a woman in a man's world: "There was a trace of vanity in the way she ran her shows. She seemed to revel in her own briskness, in her knowledge of the shuttle systems, in her use of acronyms and the strange, stilted syntax of aerospace engineers. She was decisive, and very sure of her sense for what was important and what was not" (ibid.:80).

Also, as befits any detective novel emplotment, Langewiesche's attitude toward the female principal is complex. One strain is harsh. Amid many anonymous indictments and a few named ones, Ham is the one individual singled out by name for a specific flight decision that might have made a difference. Ham cancelled a back-channel request by unnamed low-level Kennedy engineers for US Air Force photos (taken from the ground) of the condition of the shuttle's wing where the foam had struck during takeoff. Such photos might have revealed the craft's damaged condition and granted a slim possibility of repair or rescue. Langewiesche goes over some of the complex factors and events that led up to Ham's decision. Then, toward the culmination of his article, he revisits that decision—this time framed in terms of the drama and poignancy of the events that unfolded. To prepare the astronauts for possible reporters' questions concerning the foam strike, the ground communications assured the crew by e-mail that the situation had been evaluated and there was no cause for concern:

> Two days later, when Rick Husband answered the e-mail, he wrote, "Thanks a million!" and "Thanks for the great work!" and after making a little joke, that "Main Wing" could sound like a Chinese name, he signed off with an e-mail smile—:). He made no mention of the foam strike at all. And with that, as we now know, the crew's last chance for survival faded away.
>
> Linda Ham was wrong. (ibid.:85)

At other moments, however, Langewiesche is defensive of Ham and more inclined to blame the old nemesis of bureaucracy. Prior to the passage just quoted, for example, Langewiesche writes: "The truth is that Linda Ham was as much a victim of NASA as were *Columbia's* astronauts, who were still doing their science experiments then, and free-falling in splendor around the planet. Her predicament had roots that went way back, nearly to the time of Ham's birth, and it involved not only the culture of the human space-flight program but also the White House, Congress, and NASA leadership over the past thirty years" (ibid.:84).In the complex chain of decisions leading to the disaster are many made at different times and by different individuals. Certainly, more than one of these decisions could be emplotted retrospectively and raised to high literary drama by the addition of "it was a decision that would prove fateful" or some such phrase. In discussing NASA from the standpoint of bureaucracy, Langewiesche acknowledges the existence of multiple decisions and indeed a long history of decisions feeding into the *Columbia* tragedy, including points at which lines of communication were compromised and Ham was given bad advice. But novelistic strategies work differently than bureaucracy-baring strategies of exposition: a few strong actors make for a better plot than a multitude; one proximate decision is more dramatic than many distant, cumulative ones; the one last hope clumsily slipping through the fingers is more gripping than a regress of missed opportunities and sub-par performances. At any rate, the novelistic portrayal of Ham is consistently more accusatory in tone than the portrait of Ham that emerges in the context of analysis of the workings of the NASA bureaucracy.

Finally, although Langewiesche recognizes human individuals as a distinct entity, a distinct causal force in the cosmos, the fact is that his characterizations of individuals often convey less of "real" individuals than of individual "types"—as, in fact, do many literary genres, allowing readers to connect the characters in the story to those outside and already familiar. Even the terse passage (quoted above) that introduces Ham incorporates two typifications: Ham embodied NASA's arrogance, and she was an ambitious woman in a man's world. Further, there is less distance than one might expect between *detective novel types* and the great *cosmic types*—the so-called archetypes—of traditional mythologies. The generic fault to which Langewiesche repeatedly returns in his analysis—the fault characteristic of the NASA high bureaucracy generally and embodied in Ham—is what many take to be the biblical original sin—arrogance. The detective novel character type to which Langewiesche assigns Ham has a distant ancestress in the world of classical mythologies: from Pandora's jar to the biblical Eve, female seductiveness is a favorite route through which disruption enters the world.

***

The underlying separation of discourses of matter, bureaucracy, and human individuals contributes to the fascination of Langewiesche's piece in two ways. First, it creates the possibility for startling juxtapositions and shifts of frame, as well as clever transgressions in which the discourse familiar within one frame suddenly borrows the language of another. The most common transgression of this sort is the previously mentioned strategy of anthropomorphism. The inclination to attribute to inanimate matter elements of human thought and personality is apparently universal. Although typically associated with mythology and poetry, it is equally manifest in the popular presentation of science, where it can be heuristically useful as well as intrinsically gratifying.[3] Langewiesche's descriptions of science and technology are replete with clever anthropomorphic or animistic imagery. For example, as the *Columbia* approached the beginning of reentry, "On the ground so little attention was being paid that even the radars that could have been directed upward to track the *Columbia*'s re-entry into the atmosphere . . . were sleeping" (Langewiesche 2003:60).

Being in orbit is described in a way that attributes a kind of willful agency to the ground: "The orbital part of the trick is that though the shuttle is dropping like a stone, it is also progressing across Earth's surface so fast (17,500 mph) that its path matches (roughly) the curvature of the globe. In other words, as it plummets toward the ground, the ground keeps getting out of its way" (ibid.:69–70).

But most intriguing, Aristotelian material (and perhaps formal) cause is recast as efficient cause and in such a way as to confirm, quirkily, the presence of the detective story ambient. For twice Langewiesche opens a paragraph with a line more typically in detective novels spoken of the butler, namely: "The foam did it" (ibid.:72, 74). The attribution of cause here is unambiguous—the most so of all the indictments leveled by Langewiesche; and, startlingly, although directed at inanimate matter, the attribution is cast in the language of blame. The foam's guilt is intensified by the lack of any subsequent comment to provide (as he does for Ham) another, ameliorating perspective from which the foam, too, might be seen as a "victim" of NASA. It is as though Langewiesche has joyfully discovered in inanimate matter a certainty that can only be longed for in the assessment of human personalities, bureaucracies, revealing clothes, and so on. Given that the foam did it, the next logical question would carry us into Aristotle's fourth cause, the "final" cause: *why* did the foam do it?

But more dramatic, ultimately, than any such transgressions are the many instances of the discourses at odds with one another. The quantity three contains three permutations of two; each permutation—matter vs. individuals, matter vs. bureaucracy, individuals vs. bureaucracy—takes its turn on the stage.

Matter vs. human individuals: Earlier I called attention to the dramatic changeup that occurs early in Langewiesche's piece when a particular astronaut's personalized description of the view from space on final approach to landing suddenly gives way to a distanced account of the shuttle as a chunk of engineered matter leaving orbit for reentry. The concluding passages of Langewiesche's article are built around a similar transition, though this time ultimately culminating in tragedy. Specifically, in his parting novelistic interlude, Langewiesche describes, with transcribed excerpts, the banter among the crew as they (some for the first time) comment on the spectacular glowing gasses outside the window at the first stages of reentry. This is followed by an abrupt shift of perspective from inside to outside: "Outside, the situation was worse than they imagined" (ibid.:87). The remainder of the article is a respectful but distanced account, from an engineer's perspective, of the gradual and then sudden disintegration of the craft. A final phrase—"like a falling star across the East Texas sky"—suggests a remote consolation in the fact of humans having rivaled the heavens. The falling star analogy is intriguing in another sense, one Langewiesche does not mention, namely, that the term *disaster* is derived etymologically from the image of an ill-positioned star.[4]

The use of the inside-outside contrast to dramatically convey the disconnect between wishful thinking and indifferent matter is also paralleled in a passage describing a conversation in the ground control room during the breakup:

> Cain said, "Macs?"
> Kling said, "On the tire pressures, we did see them go erratic for a little bit before they went away, so I do believe it's instrumentation."
> "Okay."
> At about that time the debris began to hit the ground. (ibid.:62)

Humans, in fact, go down to many defeats in attempting to master matter. "Mere" matter is alien to humans. The alien-ness has a reliability (the so-called laws of nature) that allows us to engineer to our advantage, but that same alien-ness contributes to the stark coldness experienced when our engineering attempts meet with disaster.

Matter vs. bureaucracy: The battle of matter vs. bureaucracy, as it takes shape in Langewiesche's account, amounts to a version of the classic battle of science and religion. As noted earlier, the characteristic of bureaucracy that most fascinates Langewiesche is its tendency to engender something like religious faith among its members. Blind faith had allowed the growth of the doctrine that foam strikes do not cause mortal damage to shuttles; this item of faith ultimately necessitated a showdown between belief and evidence. A nitrogen gun normally used for aircraft "bird-strike certification tests" was employed at a late point in the *Columbia* investigation to shoot pieces of foam at shuttle panels. By this time, many felt the mystery had already been solved, and other practical factors argued against holding the test. But at this point in the narrative, Langewiesche introduces a fifth main character who briefly has a role equal to the other four: "the quiet, cerebral, earnestly scientific Scott Hubbard, who insisted that the test proceed" (ibid.:77); he is the scientist who maintains science in contrast to his colleagues' "faith." Hubbard's role also corresponds to a detective story "type": the methodical, rational forensic scientist whose role nowadays threatens to upstage that of the intuitive, plain-talking, often luddite conventional detective (in effect, the "Ducky" to Gibbs in the television series *NCIS*). The collaboration contains within itself a variation on the *agon* of man vs. machine. While Gehman's instincts lead the way, it is for Hubbard to drive the nail into the coffin: "Among the engineers who gathered to watch were many of those still living in denial. The gun fired, and the foam hit the panel at a 25-degree relative angle at about 500 mph. Immediately afterward an audible gasp went through the crowd. The foam had knocked a hole in the RCC large enough to allow people to put their heads through. Hubbard told me that some of the NASA people were close to tears" (ibid.:77). Langewiesche reports Gehman as saying, "Their whole house of cards came falling down" (ibid.).

What caused their faith to crumble? The foam did it—or, more specifically, a scientific experiment about foam and carbon did it. Part of what makes Langewiesche's account intriguing is that it is not Inquisitors of late antiquity but rather modern scientists practicing in their own elite fields who are portrayed as ruled by faith; moreover, that faith is directed toward the very objects they have created, and now are supposedly investigating, scientifically. Whether by coincidence or diffuse influence, Langewiesche's analogy between NASA's bureaucracy and a religious community is reminiscent of that offered in Thomas Kuhn's (1962) *The Structure of Scientific Revolutions*. This much-read mid-century work, through which the term *paradigm* entered mainstream vocabulary, created a long-simmering controversy by portraying scientific establishments (most notably the dogged resistance to Copernican heliocentrism) as analogous to religious communities, that is, as held together by faith rather than evidence, by believing rather than thinking.

Individuals vs. bureaucracy. Langewiesche's (2003) depiction of the battle between individuals and bureaucracy focuses on Linda Ham, but there are two fronts to this battle. One is, so to speak, the battle for the soul of Linda Ham, whom, rightly or wrongly, he portrays in part as a victim of bureaucracy. Already in the opening paragraph of his article Langewiesche broaches the theme of victimhood, with the phrase "those whose reputations have now been sacrificed" (ibid.:58–60). Sacrificed to what? Apparently, to bureaucracy. In deciding to cancel the photographs, Ham consulted the high-level managers but not the low-level engineers who had attempted to arrange for them. Langewiesche seems to fault her decision not for any breach of procedure but rather for being too strictly procedural, "a purely bureaucratic reaction" (ibid.:81). Apparently, bureaucracy's highest victory consists of making people into bureaucrats.

But Langewiesche also characterizes a second battle, that of the low-level engineers to adequately convey their concerns regarding the foam strike. On this front Ham's victimhood registers as an instance of the broader arrogance and bureaucratic insularity of NASA management that doomed such efforts from the start: "Given the obvious potential for a catastrophe, one might expect that they [the low-level engineers] would have gone directly to Linda Ham, on foot if necessary, to make the argument in person . . . However, such were the constraints within the Johnson Space Center that they never dared. They later said that had they made a fuss about the shuttle, they might have been singled out for ridicule. They feared for their standing, and their careers" (ibid.). The phrase "on foot if necessary" is interesting: like "gut" feel, it appeals to the visceral as a counter to bureaucratic insentience.

But beyond creating the possibility of clever juxtapositions, changeups, and transgressions, Langewiesche's strategy of separating and maintaining three discourses throughout contributes to a sense of intractable cosmic disharmony. Each of the three levels contains within itself a distinct sense of conflict: at the detective novel level, we have individuals struggling with their own and others' desires to create a personal place and destiny in the world; at the level of bureaucracy, we have the inevitable conflicts generated in shaping these unique individuals into a complex, functional being, a sort of super-organism with a specialized purpose lying beyond the abilities of any of them individually. The world of matter is also, in a sense, full of conflicts—for example, between heat and metal—though these are only perceived as such from the perspective of the other two levels (while from the inside, matter goes on obliviously following its own self-consistent rules).

But Langewiesche's sustaining of the three levels creates and conveys *yet another* level of conflict—a meta-level, in the current idiom—drawing to our attention a founding cosmic flaw: a fundamental disharmony of the spheres in which human life is inextricably implicated. We are both the same as, and different from, the rest of the cosmos, and that is why experiences of alignment and misalignment are profoundly true—whether perceived through space-flight telemetry that only physicists can decipher or in the triumphs or tragedies of astronaut heroes. The foundational cosmic condition that makes possible moments of sublime cosmic unity provides, at the same time, our most basic recipe for disaster.

NOTES

1. Aristotle discusses the four causes in his *Metaphysics*. See also Comte (1975); Parsons and Shils (1951).

2. Or, as one reader put it in a letter to the editor, "The *Columbia* flight did not end in tragedy because some engineer, rather than minding the computer readouts, was busy looking down Ham's blouse. I fail to understand why her dress code was included" (McKay 2004:16–18).

3. See the many examples of anthropomorphizing generally in Guthrie (1993) and of science popularizing in Schrempp (2012a).

4. On stars and disasters, see Blanchot (1995).

9

"Goodbye Spoony Juney Moon"
A Mythological Reading of Tom Stoppard's Jumpers

Sometimes idea and structure are indivisible.

Tom Stoppard (in Gussow 1996:8)

IN CHAPTER 5, I CALLED ATTENTION TO A conceit encountered repeatedly in mythological cosmologies: the assumption that there is a sympathetic resonance between the local and the cosmic, the village and the universe. It is also not uncommon to encounter mythological cosmologies that propose more finely gradated versions of such microcosmic-macrocosmic sympathies. In these, the village is situated as the smallest within a series of embedded, enlarging circles, the most encompassing of which is the cosmos. Here, too, the relationship among the micro-, the macro-, and the various "mesocosms" is generally regarded as one of reciprocating sympathies between levels. In this chapter I present a mythological reading of playwright Tom Stoppard's (1974) dramatic philosophico-scientific farce *Jumpers*, which, although showcasing modern mathematical and scientific achievement, is nonetheless staged through just such a mythological conceit.

Jumpers was first produced in London in 1972 and revived in London and New York in 2003 and 2004, respectively. From an initial intuitive sensing of their applicability to the play, I tried out aspects of a structuralist perspective developed by anthropologist Claude Lévi-Strauss for the analysis of traditional mythologies—later to find that the assumptions of structuralist method dovetail with comments Stoppard himself has made about his craft. Since there is significant chronological overlap between Stoppard's productive career and the period in which Lévi-Strauss was particularly influential in the English-speaking world—the apogee of the two also correlating with that of the era of manned space exploration—it may be that commonalities

DOI: 10.7330/9780874219708.c009

between the two intellectuals owe something to a more general intellectual sensibility characteristic of their time. Foremost in that sensibility is the notion of deep structural principles lying behind the "play of surfaces," a point I explore below and which supports a structuralist reading even amid the attention Stoppard has received from later post-structuralist and post-modern critics. Lévi-Strauss's (1971) "The Story of Asdiwal," which analyzes a traditional Tsimshian origin story, proved especially useful. Why should a method of analysis developed around a traditional Native American myth stand to reveal something about a West End theatrical farce that showcases mathematical and scientific achievement and modern space exploration? The mythic strands in Stoppard's play will emerge in the analysis that follows, but I also revisit this question and suggest more detailed answers in a concluding epilogue on the relation of myth and theater.

***

First, I turn to a summary of *Jumpers*, though the reader is ideally familiar with the full work—which can be recommended as a great read and an even greater theatrical experience. The obvious *plot* of *Jumpers*, the scenario that appears to the fore through most of the play and which the audience could be expected to emotionally connect with, is in essentials a rather conventional "whodunit" (a plot type not unlike that considered in chapter 8 and one that appears in several other Stoppard works, notably *The Real Inspector Hound* [Stoppard 1976]). Stoppard's fascination with the whodunit form seems to arise out of an abiding interest in epistemology as embodied in different possible practical habits of investigation. The who-dunit frame is filled out with characters that are caricatures, not so much of "real people" as of detective novel types. There is Dotty, a prematurely retired theatrical prima donna, neurotic and mentally coming apart; her older, anachronistic professor husband, George; an inspector (Bones) with a romantic-nostalgic soft spot for his main suspect (Dotty); an unscrupulous and politically inclined university administrator (Archie Jumper); and a secretary who is opaque, unnamed, and "poker-faced" (Stoppard 1974:14),[1] yet with a few eyebrow-raising oddities that set her up as the play's "wild card." In sum: a quirky version of the usual suspects.

The most novel twist lies in the setting: a university community, specifically a philosophy department that has certain idiosyncrasies, most notably that some of the members form an amateur acrobatic club known as the Jumpers. The play begins at a party celebrating the victory at the polls of the Radical Liberal political party. The entertainment is provided by Dotty, the Jumpers, and the secretary, who is swinging from the ceiling on a swing suspended from the chandelier, discarding clothing with each arc. Dotty, a still-stunning first lady of stage attempting a comeback, is singing songs about the moon, confusing and interfusing them but in ways that are somehow appropriate. This confusion reveals either a mental breakup or, if you will, a tendency toward a kind of mad associationism distinctive of Dotty's sensibility (and also more broadly characteristic of much of Stoppard's compositional style):

> You saw me standing in June
> January, Allegheny, Moon or July— (ibid.:20)

The audience is given an early sense of the association between the political party that has just taken power and the university philosophy department as the acrobats are introduced: the "INCREDIBLE—RADICAL!—LIBERAL!!—JUMPERS!!" (ibid. 1974:18).

When the Jumpers have succeeded in arranging themselves in a pyramid, a shot rings out, and one of the Jumpers—Duncan McFee, professor of logic—is killed; the pyramid implodes. Most of the remainder of the action revolves around an investigation into the crime, which has been anonymously reported to the police, with Dotty emerging as the prime suspect.

Dotty's husband, George Moore, professor of moral philosophy, whose greatest claim to fame lies in the fact that he is sometimes mistaken for the illustrious G. E. Moore, is a crank academic, idealistic but inflated; through most of the play, his relation to the investigation is one of obliviousness. George believes the investigator has come in response to a call that he himself had placed, complaining about the noise of the party. George is absorbed in academic concerns, among which two particularly dominate. One is his labored preparation of a manuscript, which the secretary is typing, for his presentation in this year's annual debate on the topic "Man—good, bad or indifferent?" (ibid.:46).

The other focus of concern in George's life at the moment is his pet hare, Thumper, who is missing. Thumper, along with a tortoise, Pat, and a bow and arrow, are among the paraphernalia George keeps at hand to contemplate classic metaphysical problems, preeminent among which are Zeno's paradoxes of motion and Cantor's theories about the infinite. In a department populated by "logical positivists, mainly, with a linguistic analyst or two, a couple of Benthamite Utilitarians . . . lapsed Kantians and empiricists generally . . . and of course the usual Behaviourists" (ibid.:50–51)—whose approaches to truth and ethics are permeated with the flavor of relativism, utilitarianism, game theory, and, in George's words, the conviction that "telling lies is not *sinful* but simply anti-social" (ibid.:48)—George is the lone seeker of metaphysical absolutes. The two concerns in which George is striving to emplot his own life—the preparation of the manuscript and the search for Thumper—when juxtaposed to the "real" plot, the investigation of the death of the Jumper, provide numerous opportunities for humor within the familiar device of characters talking past one another: when there is talk about the investigation, George assumes it is an investigation of the noise and disorder of the party; when theories are proposed about the death and disappearance, George assumes the talk is about Thumper.

Yet another sub- (or perhaps super-) plot, involving its own "crime," is announced early in the play and, through background projection devices, referred to throughout. The audience is made aware that in a British exploratory mission to the moon, the landing craft was damaged to the extent that it was capable of bringing back only one of the two astronauts to Earth. The situation eventuated in a skirmish on the moon over the available place. In full view of the audience on Earth, the commanding officer, Captain Scott, knocks Astronaut Oates to the ground and closes the hatch with the remark "I am going up now. I may be gone for some time" (ibid.:23).

The event is building to a focal occasion of public debate; the names Scott and Oates are allusions to the ill-fated Antarctic expedition that has come to function as a contemporary legend of altruism and courage. Among those most effected by the events on the moon is McFee, the philosopher originally slated to represent the relativistic, utilitarian—or, in George's words, "orthodox mainstream"—approach to ethics in the debate with George. Though McFee is killed at the outset, it is later revealed that McFee had been so appalled by the spectacle on the moon that, glimpsing the world he himself, in his philosophical positions, has been advocating, he decided to break with it all and remove himself to a monastery.

A particularly significant figure is Archie Jumper, chancellor of the university, who in many respects is the antithesis of George. Archie is intellectually committed to the new moral "flexibility" (ibid.:66) and is a master of its application. The new philosophical expediency pulls toward the dissolution of philosophy; skeptical of any assertions that claim to be grounded in principles larger than a particular context, philosophy divests itself of its traditional claim to investigate and provide the underpinnings of all disciplines, of knowledge in general. The leveling of disciplines finds tangible expression in Archie's role as a vaudevillian man of many hats—philosopher, doctor, administrator, legal counsel—without distinction or hierarchy.

Other than the initial entertainment and shooting, the biggest part of the "action" of *Jumpers* consists of the investigation of the murder; emphasis is less on the progress of the investigation in any technical sense than on the interactions of the characters in all of their particular quirks. The initially upstanding investigator, Bones, is filled with a kind of romantic fascination for the delicate former first lady of the stage. Archie is the ultimate "operator," attempting, and largely succeeding, to orchestrate the entire affair in the same manner that, as their leader, he directs the movements of the acrobatic Jumpers in the initial and final scenes. Dotty innocently relishes the attention and worriedly seeks a protector, first in George and then in Archie, with whom she enjoys a relationship fraught with suggestive laughter but whose nature is ultimately unclear. George is oblivious, obsessed with preparations for the upcoming debate and the disappearance of Thumper. The investigation grinds to an inconclusive halt when, through a stroke of luck (or possibly calculation; as usual, this is unclear), Archie catches the inspector in a situation that appears to be compromising. The implication is that Archie and Bones will cut a deal and that Dotty will be cleared. All of this has transpired amid a growing debate over the spectacle of the two astronauts fighting on the moon and a number of emblems of philosophy that form a sort of Greek chorus sounding the stanza: this play is about big—as in philosophical and cosmological—matters.

The scene that now brings the drama proper (the drama minus the final sequel, or "Coda") to a close involves the "wild card"; specifically, when the secretary, who has been working on George's manuscript, leaves the study, it is seen that the back of her coat is stained with a bright blotch of blood. From the stained coat, the fact (imparted to the audience unobtrusively slightly earlier) that the secretary had been having an affair with the married and lately murdered McFee, and the realization that the secretary has all along been in a position to serve as "wild card," new possibilities suddenly arise. We watch attentively as George goes over to the place where the secretary's coat had been hanging and investigates the source of the blood; he slowly withdraws an arrow he discovers from the top of the cabinet, and on it is impaled the source of the blood—Thumper. It is now clear that Thumper has been killed by the arrow that George, in the midst of contemplating Zeno's arguments against motion, had earlier released as a result of being startled by Dotty. Agitated, George steps down, alighting on his tortoise and killing him as well, thus bringing to a close the second of two main acts of the play. A coda follows, a surreal debate between George and Archie (who substitutes for the dead McFee). It is left to the audience to judge the debate.

***

I begin my analysis of *Jumpers* by elaborating on the two Lévi-Straussian themes that orient the investigation—dualistic structuring and simultaneous unfolding on multiple levels—themes emphasized by Lévi-Strauss (1971) at many points but especially in "The Story of Asdiwal." Both of these structural elements have characteristic movements associated with them, which are visible in Stoppard's play.

DUALISTIC STRUCTURING

People who have heard only one thing about Lévi-Strauss usually know that he was preoccupied with duality, particularly in the form of "binary oppositions." Lévi-Strauss's perspective turns on the notion that the mind works oppositionally, in terms of basic contrasts we encounter with particular intensity in myths: light/dark, raw/cooked, moist/dry, up/down, life/death, left/right, and so on. Yet some of his most important contributions have to do with binary structuring on a higher level: with the way traditional origin myths are built around an opposition of two entire states of the cosmos.

But there is another, related but more subtle theme in Lévi-Strauss, which indeed runs through a number of the intellectual heirs of Durkheim: that symmetry in duality is precarious at best, tending to tip one way or the other, into asymmetry or hierarchy (this theme is examined most fully in Lévi-Strauss [1967b]). The asymmetric tendency can be manifest as a typical mythological movement: the cosmos tilts from one general condition to another. A decision is made, a sin is committed, a point of connection is severed, and the cosmos moves from innocent and unborn to born and knowing—or some such version of a major changeover. Both of the opposed states continue to be entertained as theoretical possibilities, ambivalently regarded, but the two possibilities are never symmetrically actualized: the cosmos is one way and then the other.

In *Jumpers*, George, the professor, articulates a modern version of such a cosmic moral changeover, a tilting of worldview, which sets up the basic contrast the play explores: "It is a tide which has turned only once in human history. . . . There is presumably a calendar date—a *moment*—when the onus of proof passed from the atheist to the believer, when, quite suddenly, secretly, the noes had it" (Stoppard 1974:25). The same contrast reappears in the "Coda" of the play, as a debate that juxtaposes a believer's and an unbeliever's worldviews; in this debate, the unbelievers have the last word.

This structural tendency seems an entirely self-conscious strategy, for in Stoppard's self-commentary one encounters a number of variations on the theme of two plausible but contradictory formulations, nearly balanced and yet tipped one way or another. Regarding his writing in general Stoppard notes: "I don't write about heroes. I tend to write about oppositions and double acts. I identify emotionally with the more sympathetic character" (Gussow 1996:13–14).

Regarding the particular contrast between belief and unbelief that animates *Jumpers*, Stoppard says: "However preposterous the idea of God is, it seems to have an edge in plausibility. And that's really what the play's about" (ibid.:5).

Perhaps most telling, the theme arises in Stoppardian psychology: "It's just that one chooses to 'be' one part of oneself, and not another part of oneself. One has a public self and a submerged self. It's that sort of duality" (ibid.:79).

Stoppard also refers to "my dual personality" (ibid.:108) and mentions an earlier work based on the idea of a spy who can't remember which side recruited him (ibid.:50).

SIMULTANEOUS UNFOLDING ON MULTIPLE LEVELS

In "The Story of Asdiwal" Lévi-Strauss (1971) analyzes the mythical narrative of Asdiwal, a culture hero of the Tsimshian group of American Indians.

> The narrative refers to facts of various orders. First, the physical and political geography of the Tsimshian country, since the places and towns mentioned really do exist. Second, the economic life of the natives which, as we have seen, governs the great seasonal migrations between the Skeena and Nass Valleys, and during the course of which Asdiwal's adventures take place. Third, the social and family organizations, for we witness several marriages, divorces, widowhoods, and other connected events. Lastly, the cosmology, for, unlike the others, two of Asdiwal's visits, one to heaven and the other below the earth, are of a mythological and not of an experiential order. (Ibid.:7)

While the general cultural-geographic settings of "Asdiwal" and *Jumpers* have little in common, the latter also tells of events situated on several levels—indeed, approximately the levels distinguished by Lévi-Strauss. I adopt the general orientation to these levels from "Asdiwal" and adapt it to *Jumpers*. Lévi-Strauss summarizes this orientation tersely in a statement of his analytical goal, which is "to isolate and compare the *various levels* on which the myth evolves: geographic, economic, sociological, and cosmological—each one of these levels, together with the symbolism proper to it, being seen as a transformation of an underlying logical structure common to all of them" (ibid.:1). He adds that "everything happens as if the levels were provided with different codes, each being used according to the needs of the moment, and according to its particular capacity, to transmit the same message" (ibid.:14).

Analogous to the principle of dualistic structuring (with its inherent inclination toward tilting), the principle of narrative unfolding through multiple planes also has its associated characteristic movement, in the form of a movement superadded to the unfolding. This superadded movement is a movement *between* the various levels. Lévi-Strauss was typically concerned with the way irresolvable oppositions—inescapable dilemmas of existence—were displaced from one level to another. The best-known example is his claim (Lévi-Strauss 1967a:209–12) that in the Oedipus myth, irresolvable sociological dilemmas of parentage and kin behavior—overrating vs. underrating blood lines—are analogized to a dilemma portrayed in a cosmogonic myth, a myth that presents to humanity the choice of either remaining unborn or of existing defectively (i.e., as lame). There is movement: the sociological dilemma is absorbed into the cosmological one, thus making the sociological dilemma less painful and scandalous while making the cosmogonic myth, by virtue of its ability to absorb the local, more readily believable. "Hence cosmology is true" (ibid.:212). We might say that the myth thus offers the same sort of grim consolation we find when we displace a specific local misfortune to a larger principle of existence with the sentiment "that's life." For Lévi-Strauss and his followers, interest in this sort of mythical strategy centered around movements that were "upward," that is, in which domestic dilemmas were projected or displaced from the local to the cosmological. Stoppard presents a particularly interesting case for exploring moves in the opposite direction, moves that can be termed "downward."

The "Asdiwal"-inspired commentary I have to offer about *Jumpers* can be summarized in four points:

1. The goings-on in *Jumpers* can be usefully depicted in four main levels, approximately those distinguished by Lévi-Strauss but which I prefer in this case to label domestic, socio-criminological, political, and cosmological. The cosmological level designates primarily the ambient mood created by the moon exploratory mission; but Stoppard also alludes to two further spatial spheres with cosmological overtones. One of these, an ill-fated expedition to the Antarctic, corresponds to the level Lévi-Strauss designates as geographical, but it will here be considered cosmological since Stoppard's allusions to it are generally in a cosmological context. The other is the mathematical search for the infinitesimal, epitomized in Zeno's paradoxes, as an inversion of the cosmological search for the infinite. Both of these dimensions will be elaborated further later.

2. On all of these levels we have a version of the same happening. The happening can be described in terms of the duality of states noted earlier as a tilting from one general state to another, specifically in this case from a worldview of belief to one of unbelief. It occurs simultaneously on each level in a way appropriate to that level.

3. There are a number of movements between levels, either in the form of one level momentarily intruding on another or else the focus of attention being passed off from one to another. This much is similar to Lévi-Strauss's model of myth analysis.

4. As to the difference: Lévi-Strauss is mostly concerned with the upward dynamic—the passing off is from local-sociological to a higher, cosmological level, and the effect is mythic. For Stoppard the passage is more often downward, and the effect is humor or farce.

Now let us fill out these four levels, summarizing what happens on each. The main point is that on each of the four levels, approximately the same major transition takes place through the course of the play. We have on each an initial situation that can be described variously as passionate, mysterious, heroic, idealistic, and possessed of absolute standards of moral conduct, *replaced* by a situation that can be described as unheroic, "flexible," pragmatic, possessed of a "relativistic" morality and Darwinian struggle.

Domestic: Dotty tilts from George, the crackpot idealist, to Archie, the nimble pragmatist. Dotty is in a personal crisis stemming in part from prolonged episodes of mental-emotional disorder and in part from her emerging as the prime suspect in the murder of McPhee, which opens the play (to appearances she is the murderer, but the issue is never resolved definitively). Her first appeals are to George, who, unfortunately, not only fails to comprehend the situation but emerges in his own right as a minor-league killer—not of fellow humans but, through his perennial ineptitude, of small animals and magical moments. Dotty turns to Archie, who to all appearances succeeds, where George has failed, in getting her off (in both senses).

Socio-criminological: The intricacies and passions of the "whodunit," the strand in *Jumpers* most easily latched on to as the plot, are brought to an end by Archie: the ace bureaucrat does not "solve" the murder but rather "handles" it. The whodunit is not merely unresolved but, more important, is undone as a genre, for such a genre cannot exist in a world of Jumpers, where law amounts to the interests of the stronger or more clever and the sole principles are principles of management. The undoing of the whodunit genre reminds us that this genre has always depended on a competent if unkempt idealist, usually an iconoclast, as investigator—lone among the bought-off and semi-bought-off. Typically, these detective characters are world-weary and jaded in every respect except for an irrational passion for the truth (the sole remaining idealist in the world of Jumpers, George qualifies on all these accounts except competence). For the audience member who insists on a murder mystery *solved*, the pre-"Coda" conclusion does offer consolation, holding out the possibility of retrospectively reconstituting *Jumpers* as a play about the disappearance of Thumper, a matter on which we are offered closure.

Political: Society as a whole tilts toward a utilitarian government based on a "flexible" morality as the Rad-Lib Party takes control. The new government begins to rationalize the government and the economy: the minister of agriculture is made archbishop, and Archie offers Inspector Bones the chair of logic in one of his attempts to get Dotty off the hook. It is significant that the title *Jumpers* is plural.

Cosmological: For present purposes this is the most important level, and I consider it in some detail. The most obvious of the cosmological events are those associated with the just-completed moon expedition. Briefly, the world re-experiences the Copernican revolution—this time with feeling, as millions of television viewers, not just a learned few with high mathematical credentials, visualize the Earth from the moon and confront the possibility of cosmic spatial relativity.

The prime Copernican commentaries occur while Archie, as Dotty's doctor, is giving Dotty a dermatographic exam, views of her skin projected by the "dermatograph" onto television monitors like those that had projected images of the surface of moon. Dotty had earlier appropriated the goldfish bowl, inverting it on her head as a helmet and imitating the moonwalk that had just been televised. George discovers that she had allowed the goldfish to die, and this leads to George and Dotty taking a series of jabs at one another:

> DOTTY: You bloody humbug!—the last of the metaphysical egocentrics! You're probably still shaking from the four-hundred-year-old news that the sun doesn't go round *you*!
>
> GEORGE: We are *all* still shaking. Copernicus cracked our confidence, and Einstein smashed it: for if one can no longer believe that a twelve-inch ruler is always a foot long, how can one be sure of relatively less certain propositions, such as that God made the Heaven and the Earth. . . .
>
> DOTTY (*dry, drained*): Well, it's all over now. Not only are we no longer the still centre of God's universe, we're not even uniquely graced by his footprint in man's image. . . . Man is on the

Moon, his feet on solid ground, and he has seen us whole, all in one go, *little—local*. . . and all our absolutes, the thou-shalts and the thou-shalt-nots that seemed to be the very condition of our existence, how did *they* look to two moonmen with a single neck to save between them? Like the local customs of another place. (Stoppard 1974:74–75)

To summarize: the invocation of post-Copernican angst is triggered by Dotty's enacting of the moon landing. Then we have Dotty's personalized use of the Copernican metaphor as a jab at George, who expectedly responds with the proper academic version of the Copernican problem, complete with philosophical and mathematical allusions. Dotty then responds with a fascinating speech that melds the Copernican problem with the moon landing. We are aware that Dotty has been coming apart all along, one of her symptoms a sort of amalgamating slippage manifest in speech ("January, Allegheny, Moon or July"). In the context of the play, the melding might be understood as a larger version of Dotty's recurrent symptoms. However, Stoppard (through Dotty) is not the only thinker to have connected the moon landing to the Copernican revolution;[2] moreover, Dotty's amalgamations bear at least a distant resemblance to the mythic process of creative synthesis Lévi-Strauss (1970a:16–36) famously termed *bricolage*.

The first point to note about these passages has to do with gender associations: it is as if Stoppard is presenting "his" and "her" Copernican revolutions, juxtaposed. To a large extent, the two versions reflect traditional gender associations. His: the classical Copernican revolution, associated with philosophy, theology, logic, math, church history, and Western history more generally. Hers: the personal, emotional, immediate, and local (bodily reenacted by the "performer" Dotty) and also the later to arrive on the historical stage (with the moon landing), as if to call to mind the familiar theme that emotional processing proceeds more slowly and deeply than rational processing.[3] The gender associations are ancient: sun is "his," moon "hers" (in the "Coda," Dotty makes her entrance on a "spangled crescent moon" [Stoppard 1974:86]). The gender typification is reflected in George's and Dotty's respective careers and reinforced by the physical staging of the play: George's room is his study, Dotty's is her bedroom, described in stage directions as "*elegant, feminine, expensive*" (ibid.:14).

But the traditional, indeed hackneyed, gender typification is also undercut in many ways. George is the one who dotes on little animals while entirely fumbling on the human level, and Dotty is singularly incisive in cutting through George's philosophical blustering to nail the underlying point—raising the issue of whether the contrast here is in the end male-female or something more like *animus-anima* in the context of a Copernican one-two punch. Dotty is the person of power; the question is what Dotty sees in George rather than the other way around. If I am not wrong, man-of-the-mind/woman-of-the-body comedy routines typically set up (male) philosophical or scientific pretension as the butt of the joke. Stoppard is on record with some less-than-flattering comments about the pursuit of philosophy (Gussow 1996:14–16), and one does not have to try very hard to read an accusation of the charge of "sophistry" in the general parallelling of philosophy and gymnastics that runs through *Jumpers*.

"Her" Copernican reversal is played out bi-directionally. Dotty speculates about the lesson in moral relativity offered to the moon-men looking back on Earth and seeing only "the local customs of another place." But a similar perspectival revelation occurs as well in the opposite direction: humans on the earth are granted a privileged distance on themselves for the first time—a chance to view from cosmic distance the *originary* actions of humanity within a space that is pristine even if not exactly Edenic. Earth dwellers tune in to a god's-eye view of a sort of lunatic neo-original sin, committed at just the right time to inaugurate the new political order promised by the Rad-Libs.

We also find out at a later point about a specific conversion experience—a Copernican counterrevolution, so to speak—prompted by this spectacle on the moon: we hear from Crouch the servant that the utilitarian philosopher Duncan McPhee, the murdered Jumper who was to have debated George, had been thrown into a philosophical crisis by the events on the moon:

> CROUCH: It was the astronauts fighting on the Moon that finally turned him, sir. Henry, he said to me, Henry, I am giving philosophical respectability to a new pragmatism in public life, of which there have been many disturbing examples both here and on the moon. . . . But he kept harking back to the first Captain Oates, out there in the Antarctic wastes, sacrificing his life to give his companions a slim chance of survival. . . . I have seen the future, Henry, he said; and it's yellow. (Stoppard 1974:79–80)

In addition to the possible association with cowardice, yellow is an allusion to the yellow jumpsuits worn by the Jumpers, founded by Archie Jumper. The tilting of the world to a world of Jumpers seems more assured because of the death (by whose-ever hand—Archie?) of McPhee, thus quashing the counterrevolution in the bud.

There is one more Copernican twist, which, although less central to the moral issues at focus here, moves the "domestic" plot along; it is as if, with the Copernican revolution already onstage, Stoppard cannot resist playing it in terms of another, broader theme found in many of his other plays: that of the complexity and deceptiveness of appearances. The main Copernican discourse, again, takes place while Dotty is undergoing a dermatological exam by her doctor, Archie. When Dotty starts weeping after her Copernican moon speech, Archie asks, in doctorly manner, about the feelings while George predictably responds to the appeal with an academic comment:

> ARCHIE (*pause*): When did you first become aware of these feelings?
> DOTTY: Georgie. . . .
>> (*But* GEORGE *won't or can't.* . . .)
> GEORGE (*facing away, out front, emotionless*): Meeting a friend in a corridor, Wittgenstein said: "Tell me, why do people always say it was *natural* for men to assume that the sun went round the earth rather than that the earth was rotating?" His friend said, "Well, obviously, because it just *looks* as if the sun is going round the earth." To which the philosopher replied, "Well, what would it have looked like if it had looked as if the earth was rotating?" (ibid.:75)

Wittgenstein's comment reappears, in a down-to-earth version, at a later point, when George voices suspicion that more is going on between Archie and Dotty than medical procedure:

> GEORGE: Well, everything you do makes it *look* as if you're . . .
>> (*Pause.*)
> ARCHIE: Well, what would it have *looked* like if it had *looked* as if I were making a dermatographical examination? (ibid.:78)

George's earlier evasion, specifically by waxing philosophic, of Dotty's final emotional appeal to him thus returns to foil his own later attempt to reclaim Dotty, for George has provided Archie with a defense.

***

Although the moon journey affords the most obvious instance of a cosmological level in *Jumpers*, two other related strata should be noted. First, Crouch's comment about McPhee's change of heart (above) points to yet another level, which, following Lévi-Strauss, can be called "geographic." That is, through the names of the astronauts on the moon, the moon journey is juxtaposed to the famous Antarctic journey. The latter was prosaically earth-bound and aligns with an earlier morality of heroic idealism; the latter, a journey to another planetary body and inducing an experience of relativization of spatial perspective exemplifies a tilting toward the new morality of expedience.

Second, in addition to the Copernican moon journey (and the juxtaposed Antarctic journey), we find in *Jumpers* a journey of a very different kind but that is nonetheless cosmological in an inverted sense: specifically, George's quest for the absolute in terms of the outer cosmos is paralleled by equally robust puffery about mathematical regresses to the infinitesimal.[4] The latter gives rise to elaborate monologues by George on Zeno's paradoxes and to allusions to the historically long-running quest to attain a mathematical description of the circle through the device of an increasingly many-sided polygon, a venture generally designated "squaring the circle" (see ibid.:71).[5] Historically, these mathematical ambitions have carried heavy metaphysical, theological, and mystical connotations. Among other things, George is preparing to offer a solution to the problem that infinitely regressing series present to notions of God as "first term"; the difficulty is surmounted, George will declare, if God is equated not with one of the terms but with zero. Throughout, George dotes on his pets and mascots of the Zeno problem—his hare, Thumper, and his turtle, Pat.

In sum, on the cosmological level, we encounter the same tilting we have considered on the other three levels. In the frame of outward cosmology, the heroic moon journey turns into astronauts fighting one another for self-preservation. In the frame of the inverted or inward cosmology—the quest for the infinite in the form of the infinitesimal—George reverses the course of the evolution of thought, metamorphosing from philosopher to man-the-hunter: he sets his sights on the infinite but instead hits Thumper.

Two further points should be made regarding these levels. The first by now is surely obvious: besides the general parallelism of these levels, numerous resonances between them are created by specific icons or motifs. The two most obvious are the motifs of the moon and the Jumpers. Via Dotty, the moon resonates through all these levels, in such motifs as the moon landing (which coincides with the Rad-Lib victory); Dotty's entertainment career (romantic songs about the moon, sitting on a glitter moon); Dotty and the moon as a pair of heavenly bodies, further emphasized through the television monitors that project the moon's surface and Dotty's epidermis; Dotty's reenactment of the moonwalk; Dotty's impending lunacy; and indeed the general lunacy of the play.

The Jumpers theme, too, jumps around among all levels, by means of such motifs as Archie Jumper, Archie's gymnastic troupe (the "Jumpers" who jump at Archie's commands in the "Coda"), the dead Jumper at the center of the murder mystery, Archie the womanizer (jumping into bed), a world of Jumpers prophesied by McPhee, philosophy as mental gymnastics, the hopping motion of the moonwalk ("one small step . . . one giant leap"), Thumper and Pat (both names imply motion), and the Zenoian increasingly many-sided polygon, which always leaves a gap. These are only a few of the many references to the Jumpers theme. Part of the pleasure of the text stems from this proliferation of chained associations between these levels and far beyond them (how about the cow that *jumped* over the *moon*?).

A second important implication is that such inter-level associations allow the line of audience attention to be *passed off between levels*, either as momentary intrusion of one level on the other or as a more sustained transfer. From the foregoing discussion I note four examples:

(1) Early on, while George is practicing his presentation for the upcoming debate, Dotty is attempting to get his attention by randomly calling out in distress: Help! Murder! Rape! Wolves!

> GEORGE: But when we place the existence of God within the discipline
> of a philosophical inquiry, we find these two independent mysteries: the how and the why of the overwhelming question:—
> DOTTY (*off*): *Is anybody there?* (ibid.:26)

(2) Another instance of the transition from philosophical to domestic, which occurs in Dotty's comment to George about the beginning of their relationship:

> DOTTY: And so our tutorials descended, from the metaphysical to the
> merely physical . . . not so much down to earth as down to the
> carpet, do you remember? (ibid.:35)

The point has broader implications; George's carnal involvements at the time may have distracted him from writing the metaphysical treatise that might have made his career (ibid.:35–36).

(3) Dotty's dermatographic exam by Archie. This amounts to an extended "doctor joke," a genre that turns on an evasive line between a lofty scientific interest, on one hand, and a carnal or prurient interest, on the other. Within Archie's doctor routine, Wittgenstein's comment (quoted earlier) passes from cosmological to domestic.

(4) The concluding moment of the pre-"Coda" part of *Jumpers*, when George discovers that he has killed Thumper and then, in a further clumsy

gesture, also kills Pat. As noted, the entire plot of *Jumpers*—if one means by plot a line of actions that come to a conclusion—can only be seen to have been the mystery of Thumper's death.

In all these examples, we have an underlying contrast between something like mind and matter—mind represented by philosophy and academia, matter by various aspects of our bodily existence: carnal desire, emotion, illness, and, finally, clumsiness. Within this broader mind-matter opposition and resonating with the theories of motion through *Jumpers*, Zeno's paradoxes have a special place. Taken at face value, they seem to say that one should give credence to an abstract logico-mathematical proof over a common sense conclusion that is verified daily in the everyday experience of bodies (in George's words, Zeno's paradoxes "showed in every way but experience that an arrow could never reach its target" [ibid.:29]). The paradoxes are the ultimate symbol of a certain kind of hierarchy based on philosophical aloofness and contempt for the life of the philistine. The paradoxes of Zeno have the two realms built-in: the "problem," which belongs to and furthers the pursuit of abstract mathematical analysis, is traditionally introduced by allusion to a prosaic, earthy folktale about a race with a tortoise.

Considered in terms of the conventional directionality associated with the mind-matter opposition—mind as up and matter as down—the direction of all four pass-offs in the previous examples is downward, and the result is humor. Is this directional scheme a given in the nature of things or merely a convention? Regardless, the important theme is the *contrast* with the directionality of myth as theorized by Lévi-Strauss (more on this later). I suspect that reformulating any of these pass-offs in the opposite direction would result in a less humorous scenario—humor seeming to have as one of its sources deflation of the lofty, a theme that has been a part of humor theory since Aristotle (1973) proclaimed that comedy has to do with people who are "worse" and "tragedy" with people who are "better." With respect to the possibility, noted earlier, of reconstituting *Jumpers* as a play about the death of Thumper, perhaps we could add that humor flows from *plots* that are "worse" rather than "better."

The downward direction can be contrasted to the earlier-mentioned upward direction discussed by Lévi-Strauss in the context of myth—where, following Lévi-Strauss, the direction of passing off is upward: from dilemmas of local, often explicitly material existence to the realm of the encompassing and cosmological. We might be tempted to posit myth and humor as forming a continuum based on opposed directions of movement. Much could be said here; I will limit my comment to the suggestion that a more interesting approach might lie in considering the ways the two directionalities can be combined. We know that many myths, notably those based on "trickster" figures, are very funny, approaching the greatest cosmological ponderings through protagonists that are eminently carnal and clumsy. Cosmology makes the local dilemma bearable, but local humor makes cosmology bearable. The bumblings of traditional mythical tricksters would seem to be not a distant but a close reciprocal to the antic pondering of mythical questions—questions about the ultimate nature of the world and our place in it—that goes on in *Jumpers*.

But if movement between levels occurs and can be funny, we should also not lose sight of the *overall* movement in *Jumpers*: the way the various levels display simultaneously, as if to drive home through a sort of involuted repetition, the tilting of the world from one condition to another. In comparison to this tilting, the whodunit, or indeed any other plot that might be picked out of *Jumpers*, is relatively expendable other than as a device of humor: what abides is the contrast between two possible general conditions of the world.

The "Coda" consists of a surreal debate between George and Archie (who takes the place of the murdered McPhee) about those two possible general conditions. George speaks, then a seemingly totalitarian Archie sums up the new spirit, while his troupe of Jumpers jumps at his commands. Though much of the humor has been downward, the final comment, spoken by Dotty at the conclusion of Archie's seemingly triumphant speech, is upward—a funny line, though the overall effect is, as Aristotle would have predicted, more like tragedy: "Goodbye spoony Juney Moon" (Stoppard 1974:87).

EPILOGUE: ON MYTH AND THEATER

The preceding analysis began with a vague suspicion that Lévi-Strauss's (1971) analytic framework for "Asdiwal" would also prove useful in thinking about *Jumpers*. In the process of analysis, possible sources of the applicability have emerged more clearly. They have to do with various qualities of myth, which can be gathered under three foci: mythic topic, time, and mediation.

Mythic Topic

We use the term *myth* to designate stories that deal with the design of life espoused by a particular society; this is enough in itself to suggest the overlap, since both "Asdiwal" and *Jumpers* address the underlying self-conceptions of their respective societies. The story of Asdiwal tells the life story of a hero of the Tsimshian people and how his adventures reflect and contribute to the cosmic and social design of Tsimshian life. *Jumpers* is about a fundamental shift that has occurred in the value orientation of Stoppard's society. Traditional mythologies typically ruminate on values through microcosmic-macrocosmic analogies, ultimately seeking to relate the order of human life to larger structures of the cosmos. Stoppard, too, invokes levels beyond the local in various ways to reflect on the human sphere.

Mythic Time

Then there is the complex matter of "mythic time."[6] Briefly, if one looks at the ways mythologies have structured the past, there seems to be a divide. On one end of the continuum lie mythologies such as Polynesian, Greek (Hesiod), and the "emergence" stories of the North American Southwest, in which time is divided into major epochs—the first telling of the origin of the cosmos and the last the creation of human society—while intermediate epochs lay out "meso-cosmic" states between the two. Such mythologies typically employ a sort of incremental repetition: as one proceeds through different epochs—from the origin of the cosmos to the creation of earth and then of the city or settlement—the same processes of creation and destruction keep recurring, so that, for example, when one reads, in the conclusion of Hesiod's *Theogony*, about the consolidation of power under Zeus, one cannot help but feel that one has heard much of it before in the stories of Cronus or Ouranos. Or, in the Native American "emergence myths" of the Southwest, which tell of the various tribes working their way to the present surface of the earth through three lower worlds, the process of abandonment of a previous world in search of the next remains largely consistent, despite the incremental change in the content of those worlds. I term these *high-epochal mythologies*.

At the opposite end of the continuum lie low-epochal mythologies, defined by the lack (or relative lack) of clearly marked epochs. Franz Boas (1905) argued that many Native American mythologies were built around only two significant moments, a "now" and a "then," with relatively little attention given to elaborating a sequence between or, in some cases, even within these moments. In such mythologies, the adventures of a given hero might involve doings that in a high-epochal mythology would be more rigorously confined to just one epoch, as well as to that epoch's corresponding spatial sphere of action (cosmos, earth, or city). "High" vs. "low" epochal should be taken not to imply any gradient of sophistication but merely a choice made regarding the structuring of the most fluid of all substances: time. Further, the "low" and "high" of epochal may correlate inversely with other axes of comparison. *Low-epochal* would seem to correlate with *high-spectacle* theatrical value because a low-epochal value allows multiple temporal-spatial frames more readily to be "on stage" at the same moment. "Asdiwal" appears to hail from a low-epochal mythology; and that would seem to be one of the reasons why the analytic frame developed around it also meshes with Stoppard's play, for *Jumpers* utilizes spectacle to bring to life what would otherwise remain mere ponderous ideas.

High-epochal mythologies approach the development of the world in gradualist fashion, while low-epochal mythologies tend to go for onetime, rapid changeovers brought about by one or a few culture hero "transformers." The same polar tendencies operate among academic intellectual historians, for each time a scholar proposes a "revolution" in thought, counterclaims emerge of a more gradual development behind, or instead of, that revolution. No better example can be found than the idea of the Copernican revolution.[7] The Copernican revolution (and the moral shift it stands for) sits at the center of *Jumpers*, and Stoppard fascinatingly combines gradualism and revolution, though in such a way that the latter, approached with resolute Zenoianism, has more impact. A tendency grows but then produces a point: "a calendar date—a moment—when the onus of proof passed from the atheist to the believer" (Stoppard 1974:25).

As already suggested, the two kinds of temporal orientations, high- and low-epochal, would seem to contain different tendencies and potentials for performance. If one wanted not to tell or read but rather to perform a high-epochal mythology—say, Hesiod's *Theogony* (and not just the Prometheus bit we have from Aeschylus)—what sort of theatrical time frame would one adopt? The obvious approach would be sequential: three plays, or one play in three acts (Act One, Cosmogony; Act Two, Titans; Act Three, Olympians). The answer is less clear if one wants to perform "The Story of Asdiwal," whose text fails to provide such an epochally based division of the various spheres. One might opt to put all these spheres, and the possibility of microcosmic-macrocosmic play between them, on the stage all at once. This would result in something like the temporal frame of *Jumpers*, namely, a set of characters shifting back and forth between various spheres within a plot that spans only a few days, even though the distinctive characteristics of those spheres might be thought of as having originally unfolded through sequential epochs. As suggested, the reasons behind Stoppard's choice may be theatrical, specifically in the interest of spectacle; *Jumpers* is a sort of four-ring circus (a circus, in this instance, whose rings are arranged concentrically rather than adjacently). In the case of "Asdiwal," the choice is inherent in the low-epochal drift of Tsimshian mythology; but that does not preclude the possibility that this temporal drift itself may have been inspired by, or even arisen in consequence of, some broader artistic favoring of simultaneity.[8]

Finally, as an example that is interestingly both high-epochal and low-epochal, consider Richard Wagner's *Ring* cycle. The four operas of the *Ring of the Nibelungen* resemble Hesiod's *Theogony* in epochal structure, which Wagner follows in dividing the saga, mercifully, into four operas, to be seen on sequential days. But through a series of melodic riffs and motifs that reappear throughout the four, Wagner reduces the four to one repeating paradigm—in effect, merging high-epochal libretto with low-epochal melody—and one sees the logic of Lévi-Strauss's (1970b:15) claim of "that God, Richard Wagner," as the "undeniable originator of the structural analysis of myths."

Mediation

Lévi-Strauss's theory of myth is built around the idea that myths provide an intellectual tool capable of overcoming, or at least lessening, contradictions that must be faced in a society's constructing of a viable design for human life. The four levels he isolates in "Asdiwal" are each defined by oppositions, and Asdiwal's success as culture hero lies in his ability, for awhile at least, to traverse and thus mediate the conceptual and practical difficulties they pose. Asidwal's mediations are dramatized narratively through his incessant journeying: from downstream to upstream, from west to east, from land to sea, from peak to valley, from heaven to earth, from this world to subterranean world, from places of matrilocal to places of patrilocal residence. The levels in Stoppard's *Jumpers* also embody such antinomies (e.g., earth vs. heaven in the cosmic sphere; male vs. female careers and ambitions in the domestic sphere); but the ultimate focus is on a moral-philosophical debate Stoppard overlays on them and that marks a departure from Levi-Strauss's focus. Specifically, Stoppard also presents each level as a realm in which the same opposition—between a philosophy of moral absolutism and one of moral flexibility—is manifest and turns into an object of personal reflection and public debate.

Anyone at all familiar with Lévi-Strauss's work will be aware of his penchant for visually diagramming the oppositions manifest in any particular myth and also for diagramming mediating elements by locating them between the extreme points of an opposition. In *Jumpers*, we encounter another form of visualization of the midpoints between extremes, as the classic paradoxes of Zeno are enacted onstage through the arrow in flight and the race between the tortoise and the hare. In other words, in Stoppard's play, the idea of moral compromise is cleverly played out against a classic philosophical paradox that raises havoc with the very idea of a midpoint between any two positions (since any midpoint raises the specter of an infinity of them). Both "Asdiwal" and *Jumpers* end in death. Asdiwal dies when his world- and society-founding tasks come to an end and he is turned to stone halfway up a mountain. Thumper dies when actual practice "outruns" Zenoian metaphysics, as George, the fumbling defender of unmoving absolutes, fires the arrow that kills Thumper. In the case of "Asdiwal," we have the end and fulfillment of a mythic culture hero function; while in *Jumpers*, we have the possible collapse of philosophical absolutes in the modern world—a world poised to proceed into the future without them.

NOTES

1. Page references are to the 1974 Grove edition.

2. I discuss other thinkers making the connection in Schrempp (2012a: chapter 6).

3. On the other hand, in regard to another quality of emotion—fickleness—it is interesting to note how quickly public interest in the Apollo missions faded after the first moon landing. And perhaps among professionals as well; on the return journey from moon to earth after just the second lunar landing (that of Apollo 12), one of the astronauts is reported to have said, "It's kind of like the song: Is that all there is?" (Chaikin 1998:283).

4. On the relation of the infinite and the infinitesimal, see Schrempp (2012a:167–71).

5. On the venture of squaring the circle see Beckmann (1976).

6. The framework presented here is greatly indebted to previous analysis of the nature of mythic time by Franz Boas (esp. 1905) and Lévi-Strauss (1967a, 1970a: esp. chapters 8 and 9). Interesting and very compatible comments about mythic time are also found in Bronislaw Malinowski's (1961:300–305) classic work on the Trobriands.

7. For example, compare Thomas Kuhn's (1962) revolution and Hans Blumenberg's (1987) gradualism.

8. See Lévi-Strauss's (1967c) comments on the type of simultaneity known as "split representation" in Northwest Coast art. Many rituals appear to be performances of myths. I leave aside the question of what factors might distinguish myth-performance as ritual from myth-performance as theater (as we are used to thinking of Sophocles, for instance). Here it is enough to note that, whether in Native American or European traditions, theater, myth, and ritual appear often complexly intertwined.

10

Is Lucretius a God?
Epic, Science, and Prescience in De Rerum Natura

Who has such power within his breast that he could build up a song worthy of the majesty of nature and these discoveries? Who has such mastery of words that he could praise as he deserves the man who produced such treasures from his breast and bequeathed them to us? No one, I believe, whose body is of mortal growth. If I am to suit my language to the majesty of nature as revealed by him, he was a god . . . who first discovered that rule of life that now is called philosophy, who by his art rescued life from such a stormy sea, so black a night, and steered it into such a calm and sun-lit haven. Only compare with his achievement those ancient discoveries of other mortals that rank as the work of gods. Ceres, it is said, taught men to use cereals, and Bacchus the imbibing of the vine-grown liquid; yet without these things we could go on living, as we are told that some tribes live even now. But life could not be well lived till our breasts were swept clean. Therefore that man has a better claim to be called a god whose gospel, broadcast through the length and breadth of empires, is even now bringing soothing solace to the minds of men.

Lucretius (1994:129)

IN THE PREVIOUS CHAPTERS I HAVE FOCUSED on forms of science popularizing that surround us in the present world. This concluding chapter shifts the focus in one major respect: it adds the dimension of historical time. Specifically, through an experiment in anachronistic comparison, I draw in another concern of contemporary folklorists, namely, durability. Folklorists have a complicated, if not tortured, relationship with the idea of durability because, on one hand, they do not want their study limited to old-time stuff, but, on the other, some sort of persistence is part of the all-important concept of tradition. Moreover, a growing discourse of durability—envisioned less as flowing from the past into the present than from the present into the future— is emerging among folklorists and others in the mantra of "sustainability."

DOI: 10.7330/9780874219708.c010

I develop my analysis around a distant ancestor, or "patron saint," of popular science writing, first-century BCE Roman poet Lucretius. In homage to him, I open my discussion of each strategy considered below with illustrations drawn from his great work, *De Rerum Natura*.[1] Juxtaposing writers temporally distant from one another poses risks, notoriously that of whiggish historiography and hagiography. Yet anachronistic reading can also be a thought-provoking exercise, triggering important questions and insights about intellectual genealogies and principles of human cognition.[2] Indeed, many of the ideas presented here arose in the process of bouncing back and forth between contemporary writers inspired by the promise of science and works by classical Greek and Roman writers, particularly Lucretius, who were inspired by the promise of the new epistemological venture of their era, the thing called philosophy.

At roughly the time Virgil composed the *Aeneid*, Lucretius used verse epic to explain and promote the fourth-century BCE Greek philosopher Epicurus. Central to Epicurus's view is the theory of atomism, which holds that the cosmos is made up of invisible, indivisible material particles called atoms (from the Greek "un-cuttable"). Lucretius attempts to show that all processes in the cosmos, including sensation and thinking, are constituted by such atoms in interaction. But at least as important to Lucretius as the atomistic perspective is a set of moral inferences he sees as flowing directly from it. Lucretius insists that belief in the gods induces superstition, impiety, and terror in men's minds—notably fear of death and of an afterlife—and that knowledge of the theory of the regular, impersonal causation of atoms can dispel these burdens and promote human happiness and well-being.[3]

Students today reading Lucretius routinely express amazement at discovering a twentieth-century quantum thinker in first-century BCE Rome. Closer inspection in one sense deepens the astonishment, for Lucretius turns out to be a rather *late* exponent of the tradition of Greek atomism he champions (although interest in this tradition by no means ended with Lucretius). But astonishment also diminishes as deeper probing raises doubts about just how similar Lucretius's atomism is to twentieth-century science. The doctrine espoused by Lucretius is a form of physicalist philosophy, built on speculative reasoning interspersed with acute though unsystematic observations. Microscopy, telescopy, and structured experimentation are lacking. I accept in advance that the overlap with modern science is limited, although fascinating topics are there for the exploration.[4]

There remains a distinct, though more general, parallel between Lucretius and contemporary popular science writers. For like the latter, Lucretius constructs his case around a contrast of two worldviews: one based on the interactions of impersonal, material entities and forces; the other on the actions of invisible, volitional, humanlike supernatural beings. Both worldviews still exert considerable sway today, and confrontations between them are perennial (current debates over "intelligent design," for example, are merely one recent tremor along this ancient fault line). In the analysis that follows I use the term *physics* to designate the impersonal, materialistic commitment that links Lucretius with contemporary popular science writers.[5]

In presenting, in this chapter, a number of illustrations from contemporary popular science writers of the "elite" sort, I am admittedly straying from the "mass" focus that defines this book. But if I breach the topic with such writers, I uphold it in what I am looking for in them. By contrast with my previous book, in which I analyzed in detail the larger arguments of elite popular science writers, here I am sifting out from those same writers their most basic hooks and gimmicks—those appealing and general enough to have survived centuries of transformation in the paradigms and specific doctrines that constitute the history of science. My goal is not to say something new about their strategies but rather to provide a glimpse into just how old those strategies really are. Admittedly, this experiment will not reveal the precise mechanisms behind such durability—a task well beyond the scope of this book—but it does suggest some factors to consider. One can imagine the possibility of dissemination of strategies from one popular science exposition to another or, alternatively, the possibility of different expositors independently inventing the same strategies. Perhaps the most intriguing possibility lies between these two poles: a durability that inheres in the historical transmission of major folklore genres, which, however, are tapped afresh in each era as ready-to-hand molds to fill with new content. By comparing contemporary strategies with those of a prescient epic poet from two millennia ago, I sketch three principles that, I suggest, form a durable core of science popularizing—at whatever level of audience. The very fact that these general principles pervade both elite and mass science popularizing suggests as much.

Popular science writing, a hybrid genre that blends technical scientific analysis with literary aspiration, lays claim to prominent space in contemporary bookstores. While committed to explore new findings and theories, popular science writing is both formulaic—that is, built around a few basic routines—and folkloric—that is, disposed to incorporate folklore genres and idioms. In this analysis I focus on myth, legend, and epic, but virtually all verbal folkloric forms are tapped by popular science writers.[6] Why? Perhaps André Jolles was right: folklore genres form a sort of necessary bedrock of human understanding. A little less lofty answer might be that since popular science writers see themselves as offering enlightenment to humanity, they speak in forms they imagine to be appealing to the masses, often, unfortunately, bringing them off badly. In this chapter I identify and explore three basic formulas recurrent in, if not defining of, contemporary popular science writing, paying special attention to folkloric qualities:

1. Cleverly blend science and art
2. Maintain an allusive and elusive relationship with myth, legend, and other folkloric genres
3. Link theories about the physical cosmos to salient moral concerns and/or worldview.

For purposes of this analysis I restrict "popular science writing" to nonfiction works written by accredited scientific specialists who attempt to present the enterprise of science and specific scientific findings in ways that are accessible and appealing to a general audience.[7]

THE THREE FORMULAS OF POPULAR SCIENCE WRITING

The first formula of successful popular science writing is *cleverly blend science and art*.[8] The artistic component of Lucretius's *On the Nature of the Universe* is conspicuous. The work is composed in heroic verse and reflects many other epic conventions, including a multi-episodic structure based around a hero (the Greek philosophical atomist Epicurus). Epicurus's journey of mind (and by implication the journey Lucretius would have the poem's dedicatee, Memmius,[9] and other readers take) is a hero's journey, conjured up through allusions to the sort of adventures found in the *Odyssey* and the *Aeneid*. As is evident in the encomium for Epicurus (i.e., this chapter's opening epigraph), the journey proceeds from the stormy, chaotic regions of superstition to the sunlit harbor of mental tranquility.[10] Virgil's hero Aeneas takes a cosmic side trip to the underworld in the course of his voyage; Lucretius, too, offers cosmic side trips, including a thought experiment about a dart thrower who travels to the edge of the universe to settle the question of whether it is finite or infinite (Lucretius 1994:33–34 [1.967–86]). Such scenarios also allude to the agility and prowess of Epicurus's mind: "He ventured far out beyond the flaming ramparts of the world and voyaged in mind throughout infinity" (ibid.:11–12 [1.62–79]).

Supremely confident of his poetic abilities, Lucretius apprises the reader of his motives for choosing verse to present philosophy:

My art is not without a purpose. Physicians, when they wish to treat children with a nasty dose of wormwood, first smear the rim of the cup with
the sweet yellow fluid of honey . . .

In the same way our doctrine often seems unpalatable to those who
have not handled it, and the masses shrink from it. That is why I have tried
to administer my philosophy to you in the dulcet strains of poesy, to touch
it with the sweet honey of the Muses. (ibid.:32–33 [1.926–50])[11]

Moving from *De Rerum Natura* to contemporary popular science writing, one once again encounters, repeatedly, the literary work that blends
science and art. The variety of contemporary strategies astonishes. The late
Stephen Jay Gould, for example, typically opened scientific essays by citing
a specific work of (usually high European visual) art or architecture that,
he claimed, triggered this particular scientific rumination. The cathedral
of San Marco in Venice, for instance, sparks thoughts on the difference
between science and mythology (Gould 2003) and the limits of adaptationist explanation in evolutionary theory (Gould and Lewontin 1979). Titles,
subtitles, and epigrams offer another means of coating science with artistic
sentiment. Virtually all of the headings and subheadings in John Barrow's
(1995) work of popular science, *The Artful Universe*, for example, allude to
titles of literary or other artistic works.[12] "String theory," with Brian Greene
as expositor, has recently captured the popular imagination. The title of
Greene's earlier work, *The Elegant Universe* (2000), enshrines one of the
few evaluative terms—*elegant*—that has found a home in both the arts and
the sciences. In his more recent work, *The Fabric of the Cosmos* (2004),
Greene opens with a discussion of Albert Camus's reflections on the myth
of Sisyphus, thus offering a scientific on a literary-philosophic on a mythic
rumination (ibid.:3–5, 20–21).

Some works of popular science offer as their grab sober scientific reflections on the imaginative creations of fantasy or science fiction (e.g., Krauss
[1996]). Science and art converge in scientifically inspired photographic
essays; for example, Eliot Porter and James Gleick's (1990) *Nature's Chaos*
takes advantage of the fact that fractal patterns and other forms of order or
semi-order in nature are aesthetically pleasing. These are only a few manifestations of a conspicuous and near constant formula—the blending of art
and science—in contemporary popular science writing. The paucity of verse
(let alone epic verse) among contemporary popular science writers might
raise the question of whether they are less venturesome than Lucretius. The
larger context must be kept in mind: verse epic is not the "mainstream" literary genre it was in Lucretius's time,[13] and even modern poetry has for some
time had an uncertain relationship with verse. The seeming radicalness of

Lucretius's decision to present physics in verse is also lessened by the fact that, from the time of Parmenides, didacticism was a recognized function in Greek and Roman poetry.[14]

On the issue of science and verse, the most intriguing contemporary parallel to Lucretius is found in an unlikely candidate: Richard Dawkins.[15] In *Unweaving the Rainbow* (1998:ix), Dawkins argues specifically that science and poetry should mutually infuse one another. He tells us that *Unweaving* was written in response to a broadly perceived coldness in the message of his earlier book, *The Selfish Gene* (Dawkins 1989), the work that brought Dawkins celebrity. Like Lucretius, Dawkins invokes poetry as an inherently bright, pleasurable force that can alleviate the hardness perceived in his product (although for Dawkins the perceived hardness lies in the message itself, while for Lucretius it lies in the drudgery of mastering the arguments). A failed Lucretius, Dawkins (1998:xii) confesses his relative lack of poetic talent and strives for poetic effect by sprinkling *Unweaving* with poetic snippets excerpted from other authors.

Dawkins recalls Lucretius in other ways as well. For example, compared with other contemporary popular science writers (many of whom offer some sort of accommodation), Dawkins's attitude toward mainstream religion is notably dour and unforgiving—in a word, Lucretian. Both Lucretius and Dawkins present themselves as uncomprehending of this fatal human attraction. In both cases, one wonders whether poetry as a counter to cosmic sadness is not given a boost by their ruling out religion as a source of solace. Similarly, few popular science writers are as devoted to a single hero as Dawkins is to Darwin; this devotion is reminiscent of Lucretius's for Epicurus.[16] Might such advocacy, too, be prompted by the closing off of religion as a source of soteriological heroes? Even the most sanguine of popular science writers, Carl Sagan, at one point has a Lucretian moment as he converges on the same emblem—the superstitiously motivated deaths of innocent women—to epitomize the evil toward which religion can lead: Lucretius (1994:12 [1.80]) cites the sacrifice of Iphigeneia, while Sagan (1996:26) cites the burning of women as witches in seventeenth-century Europe.

But amid the similarities, an important difference stands out between Lucretius and contemporary popular science writers on the matter of blending art with science. Specifically, contemporary popular science writers often explicitly thematize the challenge of transcending the dichotomy of science and art or, more broadly, of "the two cultures," as C. P. Snow famously put it. Intent to integrate the uniquely human "embroidery of artistic activities" with the "systematic study of Nature that we call science," the mathematical astronomer Barrow (1995:1) dramatizes his task: "a great gulf seems to lie between them, shored up by our educational systems and prejudices." By contrast, Lucretius does not portray the transcending of dichotomy either as his goal or as a goal worthy in itself. However ingenious, Lucretius's blending of art and science remains ad hoc and practical: a new physics (which supports a new ethics) is the message, art is the vehicle. Contemporary readers are often struck by how untroubled classic Greek and Roman thinkers are in mixing regions of thought and experience now regarded as distinct, if not incommensurable. The fact that Lucretius claims no great credit for synthesis per se reflects a condition in which dichotomies familiar to us now had not yet gelled.

***

As suggested earlier, the relationship contemporary popular science writers seek with art is generally conciliatory, often enthusiastically so. A curious situation arises, however, from the fact that popular science writers find it necessary to maintain less conciliatory attitudes toward realms often deeply intertwined with art—specifically, mythology and religion. In most contemporary popular science writing, attitudes tend to be distributed among these three terms—*art, myth*, and *religion*—in rather predictable ways, not unlike the distribution noted in the analysis of Frank Capra's science films in chapter 6. "Art" can coexist, and may even deeply converge, with science. "Myth" or "mythology" is that which cannot coexist with science and will be replaced by it. This usage correlates with the everyday sense of "myth" as widespread falsehood ("legend" has similar associations; much of what I say about myth in the following discussion applies to legend as well). In regard to compatibility with science, religion stands midway between art and myth. Although some religious teachings (such as a literal six-day creation) may have to give way to scientific findings, more general religious ideas (such as the ultimate existence of a deity), as well as the moral insights offered in religious traditions, can coexist with—and indeed, in the view of some, form a necessary complement to—scientific understanding.[17]

Among popular science writers, then, *myth* (or sometimes *legend*) emerges as a term of choice for designating scientifically incorrect explanations. It also sometimes designates a vague nemesis, a dark force of superstition that science perennially battles. One attraction myth thus holds for popular science writers is that of the negative example, the illustration that dramatizes what we ought to believe by reference to what we ought not. But despite the dark connotations, popular science writers are not beyond invoking characters and stories from traditional myths and legends for positive illumination and edification (illustrations follow). Moreover, such writers are not beyond indulging in their own creative mythologizing and legendizing in the interest of portraying science appealingly and triumphantly. In sum, the attitude toward myth and legend in popular science writing is conflicted.

***

In light of these considerations, let us now turn to the second formula of popular science writing: *maintain an allusive and elusive relationship with myth, legend, and other folkloric genres*. Legends, particularly when raised to the artistry of epic, often also reference mythology. Throughout, Lucretius's epic poem alludes to mythological events and characters, including the generative pair of father ether and mother earth (Lucretius 1994:16 [1.250–60]). Lucretius also takes every opportunity to indulge the mythic proclivity to anthropomorphize natural processes: "Such is wind in it fury, when it whoops aloud with a mad menace in its shouting" (ibid.:17 [1.270–85]). Hence arises a longstanding quandary in critically analyzing Lucretius: how to account for the robust mythologizing in a work aimed at demolishing the mythico-religious worldview.

Classicists have generated a range of proposed solutions to the problem of mythology in Lucretius, many of which can be neither decisively confirmed nor entirely eliminated.[18] The situation in contemporary popular science writing is similar; that is, many of the reasonable conjectures about Lucretius's motives also form reasonable conjectures about the motives of contemporary popular science writers. Speculations span psychological factors (such as the possibility of internal conflicts within these authors), dimensions of textuality (including, notably, the variety of ways mythology can be invoked with non- or quasi-literal intent), and rhetorical strategy (e.g., the use of enticements with intent to "bait and switch"). In the case of contemporary popular science writers at least, the mythologizing seems to be impressionistic, groping, even subliminal—myths thinking themselves through scientists.[19] I suspect that in many cases such writers would not be able to give an entirely coherent and consistent account of their mythologizing motives. Nevertheless, three possibilities seem especially likely: proselytizing comparison, metaphor, and science heroizing.

Proselytizing Comparison

Book One of Lucretius's poem opens in praise of Venus: "Mother of Aeneas and his race, delight of men and gods, life-giving Venus, it is your doing that under the wheeling constellations of the sky all nature teems with life" (ibid.:10 [1.1–20]).

The rapturous passage announces the topic of the first book (and in many ways of the entire work), namely, the remarkable fertility and regeneracy on display in the workings of nature. This mythologically informed passage, however, is followed by an elaborate and technical account—from the perspective of atomistic materialism—of those same qualities of nature, offering along the way various proofs of the correctness of the atomistic view.[20] For example, the theory of indestructible atoms offers a mechanism for the continuity of nature evident in the fact that like only begets like. Without this, "Men could arise from the sea and scaly fish from the earth, and birds could be hatched out of the sky. Cattle and other farm animals and every kind of wild beast, multiplying indiscriminately, would occupy cultivated and waste lands alike. The same fruits would not grow constantly on the same trees, but they would keep changing: any tree might bear any fruit" (ibid.:14 [1.154–91]).

One can suspect that the mythological view of the world forms the target here; anthropologist Claude Lévi-Strauss (1967a:203) comments that "it would seem that in the course of a myth anything is likely to happen."[21]

One obvious motive for such juxtapositioning, then, is that it facilitates the comparison of two worldviews; Lucretius leaves no doubt as to which view deserves final credence. If one compares *De Rerum Natura* to the Capra science films discussed in chapter 6, one encounters a form of persuasion different in particulars but identical in basic strategy. Capra's films are full of studio-animated "mythological" accounts of the workings of nature (a smiley sun, a toga-draped heart, little men inside a brain) juxtaposed with scientific illustrations of the same phenomena based on realistic photography. Once again, while the mythological account may be the popular draw, the films deliver clear judgments on which is real (recall Mr. Sun's "of course what I really am is a star, an average, everyday type of star"). Such juxtapositioning is also encountered frequently in contemporary popular science writing. For example, Richard Dawkins (2003) offers a mythico-religious (or pseudo-mythico-religious) New Age explication of crystals and follows immediately with a scientific explication. Acknowledging that the New Age explication exercises a limp attraction, Dawkins is betting that the audience can be won over by the analytical depth, detail, and acuity the scientific account has to offer. The latter view ends up mocking the former: "But isn't it all—crystal ball gazing, star signs, birth stones, ley-lines and the rest—just a bit of harmless fun? If people want to believe in garbage like astrology, or crystal healing, why not let them? But it's so sad to think about all that they are *missing*. There is so much wonder in real science. The universe is mysterious enough to need no help from warlocks, shamans and 'psychic' tricksters" (ibid.:43).

Metaphor

The atomistic theory Lucretius champions harkens back to the so-called Greek miracle, the period beginning around the sixth century BCE that witnessed a rapid rise of various philosophical schools, accompanied often by skepticism toward myth. "Myth," as the foil of philosophy, took on connotations of epistemological inferiority. But the skepticism was also accompanied by new roles for myth, including the use of myth-like scenarios to, metaphorically, dramatize the emergence of philosophy.[22] Plato's *Republic*, a work that offers a scathing attack on the traditional stories of the gods told by Hesiod and Homer (Plato 1985:72–75 [377–78]), also offers the famous allegory of the cave (ibid.:209–12 [514–17). This allegory portrays the mind first catching a glimpse of the higher truth of philosophy through a scenario—entrapped humans escaping from the dark into the light—that inspires many origin myths.[23]

For his part, Lucretius says: "If anyone elects to call the sea Neptune and the crops Ceres and would rather take Bacchus' name in vain than denote grape juice by its proper title, we may allow him to refer to the earth as the Mother of the Gods, provided that he genuinely refrains from polluting his mind with the foul taint of superstition" (Lucretius 1994:53–54 [2.650–60]).

Following this logic, Venus can be retained as an evocative symbol for the generative power of nature, a force that clearly leaves Lucretius in awe. And Lucretius's allegory of the birth of Epicurus's philosophy, in the form of a voyage, taps into some of the same imagery that characterizes Plato's cave, notably the passage from darkness to light. Although metaphor can also be heuristically useful in depicting and explaining even the subject matter of the new physics, its most powerful use lies in leading humans into the new enterprise by supplying a human context, meaning, and tone, making the new enterprise into an adventure.

Analogously, metaphorical-allegorical use of mythological imagery in contemporary popular science writing serves to dramatize the significance of the enterprise of science. Indeed, some of the most hard-boiled contemporary messengers of science serve up some of the heartiest mythological brew. Edward O. Wilson (1998:7, 34–35) invokes mythological figures such as Icarus and Prometheus and, even more venturously, offers a pastiche of shamanic imagery gathered under the rubric "Ariadne's Thread" (from the Greek myth of the Cretan Labyrinth and Minotaur) to explicate his view of scientific method. The latter excursus sits in the middle of Wilson's *Conscilience* (ibid.: chapter 5), a work often perceived as a manifesto of reductionist, hegemonic science.

Consider also the Committee for Skeptical Inquiry (CSI), discussed in chapter 3, a society of contemporary rationalists intent on debunking scams, from Ponzi schemes to faith-healing artists, to which their contemporaries have fallen prey. Popular science writers such as Stephen Jay Gould, Carl Sagan, Marvin Minsky, and Steven Pinker are lionized by this group and are frequent contributors to its literature and symposia (e.g., its magazine *Skeptical Inquirer*). "Myth" for these skeptics is a generic label of the false, yet CSI's publishing venture is called Prometheus Books. The founder and chairman of the organization and of Prometheus Books, Paul Kurtz, writes: "The 'patron saint' of humanism is the ancient mythological character Prometheus, who challenged the gods on high, stole fire, and bequeathed to humankind the arts and sciences of civilization—so that we need not huddle in fear and tremble in caves, as did primitive men and women, but that we might go forth, taking destiny into our own hands, and overcoming the limits of our animal natures" (Kurtz 1997:9–10).

The two possible motives for science mythologizing discussed thus far, "proselytizing comparison" and "metaphor," can work in synchrony. The reader is enticed by the power of myth into a scheme at loggerheads with mythical explanation. But the legitimization of metaphorical reading simultaneously provides the reader with a new use for, hence a way to salvage, the beloved old order. This legitimization can be seen as a variation on the tradition of allegorist interpretation of mythology (see Brisson 2004), which already exerted influence in Lucretius's time.

If Lucretius's rich use of mythology has produced bafflement, it is worth noting that certain works of contemporary popular science similarly baffle. For example, why does Stephen Hawking conclude *A Brief History of Time*, a work with no need for the hypothesis of God, by commenting that if we can scientifically discover why the universe exists, "then we would know the mind of God" (Hawking 1988:175)? This notorious conclusion has fueled a stream of speculations, ranging from sublime (hints of a submerged spirituality?) to cynical (to boost sales?). Among other things, images of "the mind of God" and "god's-eye view" have become, in secular contexts, rather standard metaphors for the ideal of a perfect and complete science. This image and those discussed previously together metaphorize the full career of science: Prometheus signifies the inspiration, the Labyrinth the method, the mind of God the goal.[24]

Even the possibility of cynical motives in contemporary popular science mythologizing invites comparison with Lucretius. As noted earlier, Lucretius is candid about his willingness to sugarcoat his message. A much more radical disingenuousness is suggested by the possibility that Lucretius was influenced by the tradition of metaphrastic poetry (see Godwin 1994:xxvii), a tradition in which poets demonstrated their compositional virtuosity by poetizing subjects of marginal concern (such as farming tips) to their listeners. The ugly thought arises that contemporary popular science writing is a cynical genre—any noble intentions are buried under the pursuit of personal celebrity and a willingness to give the masses literary bread and circuses in return for support for science. For either Lucretius or contemporary popular science writers, the charge of ultimate disingenuousness is extreme, although vulnerability to this defect is inescapable in any attempt to popularize esoteric learning, particularly when the audience actively seeks bedazzlement.

Science Heroizing

The figure of Prometheus can also serve to illustrate one other form of mythological intrusion in popular science writing. Prometheus is the type of figure mythologists call "culture heroes": heroes whose contributions form the basis for a truly human way of life, who mark the point at which humanity begins. The contribution may be practices or technologies—social norms, agricultural techniques, clothing, or fish weirs—that distinguish one human group or way of life from others and humans as a species vis-à-vis other species. Cross-culturally, fire is one of the more recurrent gifts bequeathed by culture heroes.[25]

As noted, proponents of science sometimes invoke well-known mythological culture heroes to dramatize, metaphorically, the significance of science. More interesting, attempts to glorify particular intellectual endeavors inevitably lead to the transformation of actual historical figures into something resembling mythical culture heroes. In the third century BCE, the Greek Euhemerus proposed that mythico-religious systems originated through a process in which illustrious humans came to be thought of as gods (the theory is now known as "euhemerism"). In speaking in the same breath of the achievements of gods and great humans (see the chapter's opening epigraph), Lucretius may be alluding to something like Euhemerus's theory of mythogenesis. If so, Lucretius's nomination of Epicurus involves Lucretius in the very creation of mythology (according to a then highly regarded theory of how this happens). However, Lucretius's particular contribution to the creation of mythology simultaneously undercuts the status of mythology in two (ultimately contradictory) ways: by raising to the highest mythico-religious level the founder of an alternative to a mythico-religious understanding of the world and, more broadly, by laying bare—indeed, by actively demonstrating—the all-too-human process through which claims of divinity originate.

But apart from the specific processes asserted in the Euhemerist doctrine, the human need for heroes is attested universally, and the nomination of heroes is inevitably accompanied by patterns and rhetorical strategies well documented in the study of traditional myths and legends. These patterns and strategies show through no less when the heroes and the heroizers are modern scientists. For example, as in many mythologies, there is a preference for heroes of contemporary science that, in the manner of Prometheus, are wayward, quirky, and prankish—in other words, tricksters (Richard Feynman is perhaps the most vivid recent exemplar [see Feynman 1985]). Also, one of the most successful formulas of science heroizing rests on a triad of heroes, recalling folklorist Axel Olrik's (1965) law of threes (or the claim that in Western folk narratives significant events, such as the overcoming of obstacles, occur in patterns of three). As was noted in motivational speaker Michael Gelb's use of science heroes in chapter 2, the most influential triad of science heroes is that advocated by Freud (1964:284–85): Copernicus in the realm of the physical cosmos, Darwin in the realm of biological life, and a third hero in the realm of psychic life (as noted earlier, this third hero is modestly left unnamed by Freud). Each of these heroes, claims Freud, delivered a distinct blow to naive human "self-love" (ibid.:284). Freud's triadic formula has been picked up by popular science writers, appearing repeatedly and with the same sorts of textual variations one can trace in the process of dissemination of any folkloric form.[26]

Yet another characteristic that links some scientific culture heroes to mythological culture heroes, as well as to holy people and saints of traditional religious legend, is the theme of functional disconnection from the practical world. There is sacred irony in the fact that those who would give us the higher truth about the physical cosmos have trouble getting around in that cosmos. Plato passes on a story about the presocratic Thales: "A witty and attractive Thracian servant-girl is said to have mocked Thales for falling into a well while he was observing the stars and gazing upwards; declaring that he was eager to know the things in the sky, but that what was behind him and just by his feet escaped his notice" (quoted in Kirk, Raven, and Schofield 1983:80).

Following a reference to astrophysicist guru Stephen Hawking's degenerative physical condition, the closing sentiment offered in a popular biography is: "He is our planet's most fully developed cerebral creature, a man who lives to think" (Boslough 1989:117). It is as if science carries forward, in the guise of body vs. mind, the earlier zero-sum game of religious asceticism: that of body vs. spirit. Even though Hawking's scientific vision has no use for mind-body dualism, this doctrine has worked well for heroizing Hawking.[27]

But there are also ways in which scientific culture heroes differ from their traditional mythico-religious counterparts, and Lucretius's heroizing of Epicurus lies between the two. The quintessential culture heroes of science, though retrospectively constructed, are cast within a temporal framework that looks forward. The true gift of Copernicus thus is not a specific finding about planetary orbits but rather the removal of an impediment—narrowly, the geocentric cosmos; broadly, our anthropocentric proclivities—that had frozen the progress of knowledge. Through Epicurus's philosophy, Lucretius, too, seeks the removal of an impediment, specifically the anxiety-ridden worldview of traditional religion. But in striving to remove this impediment, the benefit Lucretius seeks is personal moral transformation, not the further progress of research and knowledge or the technological benefits that will flow from them. Epicurus's philosophy, in Lucretius's portrayal, emerges more as a completed, timeless doctrine than a "research program"; in this respect, Lucretius's Epicurus is more the mythico-religious than the scientific culture hero. The relation Lucretius postulates between anxiety and religion offers another, related counterpoint to the present: Lucretius proceeds as though he thinks his audience will need little convincing that religion is a source of anxiety in need of solace, while many contemporary popular science writers proceed as though their greatest challenge lies in having to ask their readers to let go of some of the forms of solace offered by religion—not to mention the perception of science itself as a source of anxiety.

***

Mythology and legend are replete with morals and moral musings; by incorporating these genres, Lucretius fosters the mood of moral inquiry that permeates and motivates his explication of the physical doctrine of atomism. Physics is made more compelling by being tied to questions about the meaning of life and the way we should live. A third formula of contemporary popular science writing is *link theories about the physical cosmos to salient moral concerns and worldview.* While few contemporary popular science writers would claim the province of moral reasoning solely for science, nearly all of them attempt to show the relevance of science and specific scientific findings to prominent contemporary moral concerns.[28] While striving to blend science and art, popular science writers thus also strive to interrelate the realms of fact and value. The moral insights they proffer in the name of science are often set out as challenges to the moral wisdom offered by religious and humanistic traditions, along with the suggestion that the latter can be improved or at least put on a firmer base.

The ways popular science writers strive to offer moral insight are many. The most basic claim is that better understanding of the world offers firmer ground from which to make moral decisions. Greater maturity is promised in return for accepting hard truths over childish fantasies.[29] Popular science writers often inject a personal, anecdotal angle that is sometimes reminiscent of self-help literature.[30] Certain phrases from popular science literature have taken on a life of their own in subsequent literature and debate, including Hawking's earlier-mentioned "mind of God" comment and a line from the closing of Steven Weinberg's *The First Three Minutes*: "The more the universe seems comprehensible, the more it also seems pointless" (Weinberg 1984:144).[31] At least among the popular audience, the passages that achieve such stature are not about mathematical equations but rather about the *meaning* of the cosmos and human existence—confirming that what many people want out of science, and what many popular science writers are willing to proffer, is moral insight. That aspiration has a distinctly Lucretian ring.

But the most intriguing strategy of connecting contemporary science with moral concerns involves a principle that lies at the heart of many traditional mythologies, namely, the idea that the structure of the cosmos offers templates for the design and conduct of human moral life. Mythology shows no shame in overtly positing parallels between macrocosm and the variety of microcosms: society, village, individual. In Lucretius's atomistic physics, too, we encounter the strategy of drawing cosmically backed morality lessons. A prime example concerns the proper attitude toward pleasure. The pleasure doctrine Lucretius offers rests on a principle of moderation, the latter based on the idea of Epicurus that once a need is satisfied, no greater pleasure can be obtained. Hence it is fruitless, for example, to attempt to secure lavish clothing once the basic need for clothing is satisfied:

> To the earth-born generation in their naked state the lack of skins meant real discomfort through cold; but we suffer no distress by going without robes of purple, brocaded with gold and extravagant figures, so long as we have some plebeian wrap to throw around us. So mankind is perpetually the victim of a pointless and futile martyrdom, fretting life away in fruitless worries through failure to realize what limit is set to acquisition and to the growth of genuine pleasure. It is this discontent that has driven life steadily onward, out to the high seas, and has stirred up from the depths the surging tumultuous tides of war. (Lucretius 1994:165 [5.1423–49])

Lucretius implies cosmic backing for the principle of limitation, for his injunctions about pleasure recall his descriptions of the physical cosmos. The implication is that our reasoning about the physical cosmos and our moral reasoning share the same defect: the failure to recognize that everything has limits. Atomism is the corrective, confirming that not just anything can happen—first and foremost, as regards what can beget what, but in other ways as well.[32] Epicurus is praised as the cosmic traveler who "proclaimed to us what can be and what cannot: how the power of each thing is limited, and its boundary-stone sticks buried deep. Therefore superstition in its turn lies crushed beneath his feet, and we by his triumph are lifted level with the skies" (ibid.:12 [1.74–79]).

The argument passes seamlessly from rectification of our understanding of the physical cosmos to rectification of our moral situation. Further, "If men saw that a term was set to their troubles, they would find strength in some way to withstand the hocus-pocus and intimidations of the prophets. As it is, they have no power of resistance, because they are haunted by the fear of eternal punishment after death" (ibid. [1.103–12]).

In sum, Lucretius's arguments suggest a cosmic deduction: the cosmos sets physical limits to everything, *therefore* we should base our moral conduct as well on the recognition that everything—including pleasure, suffering, and the term of life—has limits.

In his earlier-mentioned contemporary work *The Artful Universe*,[33] John Barrow (1995) parallels Lucretius in suggesting a cosmic backing for a moral principle; there is even a degree of overlap in the particular moral principles at focus in the two thinkers. Addressing the "nature" vs. "nurture" controversy that raged throughout the twentieth century, Barrow argues that the arts and humanities have gone too far in privileging "nurture" over "nature" in conceptualizing art and culture. The sciences, he says, have come to accept complexity and contingency; the humanistic disciplines should now reciprocate by recognizing the operation of laws of nature within enterprises typically regarded as constrained only by cultural norm. In an attempt to shift our view of art in the direction of "nature," Barrow presents evidence of the operation of universal constraints in art. One line of evidence is a purportedly universal preference for savanna-like tree density in landscape art, which Barrow relates to the physical context of human biological evolution (ibid.:91–101); another is a preference for bilateral symmetry, which Barrow sees as an artifact of our predator-alert brain wiring (bilateral symmetry being a signature of living things and hence of potential predators) (ibid.:104–05).

But Barrow does not present these arguments in isolation; rather, he rests them upon cosmological scaffolding. Specifically, Barrow opens his discussion about constraint in art with a discussion of some of the more general laws of nature that constrain not only the production of art but the entire cosmos. He discusses first some of the parameters that define the possibility of the existence of any physical body in the cosmos (i.e., the range within which matter neither flies apart nor collapses into black holes; see ibid.:48–54). He then moves to those narrower parameters that define the possibility of life (such as the conditions necessary for a planet to have an atmosphere). Finally, he moves to the still narrower parameters that define the conditions within which consciousness, culture, and art might arise;[34] only at this point does Barrow discuss the conditions of our biological evolution and the way they have imprinted themselves, he claims, universally on human aesthetics. While the first two sets of parameters, those forming the basic conditions of all matter and all life, are related only rather distantly to the "nature-nurture" debate, Barrow's presentation nevertheless conveys the feeling of a progressive closing in toward, and hence a cosmic backing for, his claims about art. Art must be contextualized in the cosmos, and the cosmos is defined by constraint: *therefore* the absence of defining constraint in art would be out of character with the cosmos. Like Lucretius, Barrow finds in impersonal, cosmic regularity a tonic for the moral doctrines that torment people's minds. Like Lucretius, Barrow—and, in varying degrees, most popular science writers—extrapolates beyond, often far beyond, specific findings or physical descriptions and attempts to present something like a cosmically based moral lesson or worldview.

RETURNING TO THE CAVE

In considering the powerful image of leaving the cave, it is easy to gloss over the attention Plato gave to the plight of the escapee *upon return* (Plato 1985:211 [516–17]). The individual who believe s/he bears a higher message faces the task of selectively reversing the course of his/her own enlightenment to communicate with the dwellers of the dark. But those who claim a higher message sometimes attract disciples who adopt the role of mediator. Such a figure was Lucretius, and many contemporary works of popular science writing are similarly composed specifically to explicate the theories of one particular champion—Darwin among the most popular.[35] In an era skeptical of world-historical meta-narratives, popular science writing remains a holdout, voicing confidence that science will give us a powerful new epic that is at once historical and cosmological and which can be appealing to all of humanity. Departing from the more typical scientific usage (discussed earlier), Edward O. Wilson (1998:265) describes the goal of science as "a new mythos." No less than Lucretius, Wilson is confident of the poetic potential that lies in the new venture: "The true evolutionary epic, retold as poetry, is as intrinsically ennobling as any religious epic.

Material reality discovered by science already possesses more content and grandeur than all religious cosmologies combined" (ibid.).

But not everything in "the new epic of science," as Martin Eger (1993) terms the emerging vision, will be entirely new—least of all the idea of an epistemologically superior epic set against the outdated ones of religion and mythology. If I am right, the basic literary-rhetorical strategies that propel the florescence of popular science writing in our time, including the very disposition to render the history of science *as epic*, are in evidence already in the work produced by Lucretius millennia ago. Now as then, these strategies draw their greatest inspiration from the worldview they seek to supplant. Facilitated by widespread literacy, energetic promoters, and the unprecedented media reach and media literacy of our time, it is now possible to believe that the souls not only of society's elite but of all humanity might finally be swept clean.

Two millennia ago, Lucretius managed to largely define the present situation of science and the popular audience—not so much at the level of specific doctrines but at the level of everyday resistance and strategies to counter them. The tension implicit in Lucretius's project, and the folklorically rooted expressive forms tapped to ameliorate that tension, are aspects of human experience we may never transcend. The *enormity* of Lucretius's project and the very *prescience* of *De Rerum Natura* make it difficult to resist entertaining the notion about Lucretius that Lucretius voices concerning Epicurus: that he must be a god.

NOTES

1. Latham, whose translation I follow, renders the title *On the Nature of the Universe.*

2. See my discussion of cross-cultural/temporal comparison in Schrempp (1992:5–6).

3. Lucretius did not deny the existence of gods, only that they would have an interest in human affairs: "it is essential to the very nature of deity that it should enjoy immortal existence in utter tranquility, aloof and detached from our affairs" (Lucretius 1994:53 [2.645–50]). He follows Xenophanes and Plato, who insist on purifying divinity of anthropomorphic content.

4. For example, science writer John Horgan (1997:17) suggests an analogy: "Quantum mechanics, which unveiled a probabilistic element, a Lucretian swerve, at the bottom of things, was an enormous surprise; God does play dice." The doctrine that in falling some atoms swerve is a vague notion from Epicurus that Lucretius uses to account for free will amid atomistic determinism. Not all contemporary scientists, however, would accept the idea that quantum uncertainty constitutes the ontological ground of, or even has anything to do with, free will.

5. In neither case does the perspective preclude the existence of gods, only their direct, ongoing intervention in the workings of nature.

6. One exception may be folktale (*märchen*), which perhaps is excluded from science exposition because of its deep association with fantasy. Richard Dawkins (2005) utilizes the

format of the *Canterbury Tales* as a frame for elaborating the history of biological evolution. Many folklore scholars regard epic as a sort of illustrious cousin of legend; that is, epics are historical legends rendered artfully, typically in verse. Hence in the following analysis I often treat epic in the context of legend.

7. Not all usages would be so restrictive. The line between popular science writing and other genres—such as science fiction or even some forms of "self-help" and "New Age" literature—can become quite blurred. A bewildering variety of genre terms (including "popular science," "science writing," "science journalism," "scientific essay," and "expository science") surrounds the sort of works I consider in this essay.

8. In addition to the three I single out, one other formula might be noted, specifically, simplification of scientific data and analysis (particularly of mathematics). But since many forms of science exposition (notably textbooks) involve simplification, this characteristic is not diagnostically useful. Other characteristics typical for the genre but peripheral to its actual content could also be cited, for example, the prominent display of authors' academic credentials.

9. Memmius is widely thought to be a real individual of Lucretius's time.

10. The opening passages of the six books also reflect the transformation Lucretius would have his readers undergo. Book One opens with an invocation to the goddess Venus (discussed later). Book Two opens with one of Lucretius's most powerful portrayals of the sad and anxious lot of humanity, a passage permeated with the image of tempestuous weather, shipwreck, and battle. The remaining books open with praise for Epicurus and his teachings. *De Rerum Natura* concludes with the depiction of a plague that overtakes Athens and forces a spate of burial rituals (note that the *Iliad* [Homer 1989] also ends with a funeral—that of Hector). Hardly a sunlit harbor, the plague holds out a jarring conclusion; yet, to face a horrific death scene with equanimity would be an appropriate "final exam" in the course of philosophy Lucretius offers (see Gale [1994:224–31] for a discussion of theories of the significance of the plague). The final book also deals with meteorology; thus Lucretius attempts to undercut, adjacently, the superstitions that surround, on one hand, people's greatest fear and, on the other, the greatest symbol of the fearful life, namely, tempestuous weather.

11. A nearly identical passage occurs near the beginning of Book Four (Lucretius 1994:95 [4.10–30]).

12. Among Barrow's chapter subheadings are "A Room with a View," "Gravity's Rainbow," "Of Mice and Men," "War and Peace," and "Far from the Madding Crowd." See also the table of contents of Ferris (2001).

13. Many of our translations of Greek and Roman epics (including the translation of Lucretius I draw upon) dispense with the versification.

14. In her study of classical sources, Volk (2002:1) introduces the idea of didactic poetry with the comment "to our feeling, it is a contradiction in terms."

15. A few decades ago the scientist-poet Loren Eiseley would have been the obvious focus; currently, he is less in vogue than Dawkins.

16. In the opening paragraph of *The Selfish Gene* Dawkins says, "Living organisms had existed on Earth, without ever knowing why, for over three thousand million years before the truth finally dawned on one of them. His name was Charles Darwin" (Dawkins 1989:1).

17. Contemporary popular science writers broadly follow in the wake of the Greek thinkers (notably Xenophanes and Plato) whom Lucretius follows in attempting to excise anthropomorphic content from the idea of the divine. However, two differences particularly stand out. First, to the extent that contemporary popular science writers reject direct, ongoing divine intervention in nature, they generally do so out of a commitment to naturalistic

explanation rather than a concern to avoid the alleged impiety of anthropomorphic portray-als of gods. Second, contemporary thinkers more explicitly invoke dichotomies of social and intellectual function: "To cite the old cliches, science gets the age of rocks, and religion the rock of ages; science studies how the heavens go, religion how to go to heaven" (Gould 1999:6).

18. Gale (1994) and Volk (2002) offer overviews of theories about Lucretius's mytholo-gizing. Gale's (1994) fascinating study advocates a coherent Lucretius and is put forward in opposition to what she regards as a longstanding tradition of regarding Lucretius as torn in opposed directions. In contrast to most contemporary popular science writers, Lucretius was an artist first, and this may be one reason to suppose that his literary strategies were more considered than those of many contemporary popular science writers. On the other hand, coherence can be a gift the living bestow on the dead.

19. The notion of myths thinking themselves is adapted from Lévi-Strauss (1970a:12).

20. In addition, at later points Lucretius speaks somewhat less rapturously about Venus, portraying her as a source of torment (e.g., Lucretius 1994:122 [4.1050–75]). In the course of his poem, Lucretius in effect seeks to replace one hero with another. Book 1 opens in praise of Venus, in Book 4 she is denounced, and Book 5 opens by (rhetorically at least) deifying Epicurus (i.e., the epigraph at the beginning of this chapter).

21. A quick overview specifically of nature's discontinuous fertility as attested in world mythology is available in Stith Thompson's (1955–58) world survey of folk narrative, under the category "miraculous birth." Humans or supernatural beings are born from every con-ceivable body part as well as from a variety of plants (the T543 series), minerals (the T544s), the ground (T545), and water (T546), including hailstones (T546.2) (ibid. 5:396–97).

22. In addition, various schools of allegorism claimed that highly esoteric teachings could be decoded from traditional myths. These schools need not concern us here.

23. For example, the themes of transition out of spatial confinement, and from dark-ness to light, figure centrally in many origin myths of the separation of sky and earth (see Numazawa 1984:186), as well as in Native American stories of "emergence" from the earth (e.g., Courlander 1987).

24. Moreover, in *The Fabric of the Cosmos*, Greene (2004:22) adds a fourth aspect of the career of science by tweaking the myth of Sisyphus to dramatize science's slow but sustained progress: "The rock of our collective scientific inquiry . . . does not roll down the mountain. Unlike Sisyphus, we don't begin from scratch. Each generation takes over from the previ-ous . . . and pushes up a little further."

25. The acquisition of fire sometimes designates both the dawn of humanity and the special character and prestige of one clan (regarding the latter, see, for example, the story of the Hopi Fire People in Courlander [1987:19]). The classic survey of myths of the origin of fire is Sir James Frazer (1930).

26. For example, in two recent works I consider elsewhere in this chapter, one finds varia-tions on Freud's triad: in Gould (1997:17–19) and Dennett (1996:206–7; cf. 18–23).

27. Further examples of the heroizing of Hawking can be found in White and Bribben (1992) and of scientists in general in Nelkin (1995).

28. Eger (1993:189–90) elaborates on a "P-S-P" (philosophy-science-philosophy) for-mat that he sees as characteristic of some recent works of science exposition: "Certain human or social problems are posed and related to some aspect of science; that science is then expounded in a lengthy technical or quasi-technical section, and the work ends with the original philosophical problems to which solutions or responses are now offered on the basis of the scientific content just presented." Eger restricts his analysis to a type of serious

science exposition he sees as differing "qualitatively" from mainline popularization. I am inclined to see the P-S-P format as one variation on the quest—at least as visible, if not more so, at the vulgar end of popular science writing—to interconnect science with broader human moral concerns.

29. See, for example, Dennett (1996:17), who portrays the theories of Darwin in opposition to the sentimentalism of the childhood song "Tell Me Why."

30. Successful self-help writers often manage to convey a one-to-one relationship with the reader even in the midst of highly generic, "best-selling" advice. Similarly, for example, Stephen Jay Gould uses a sort of generic "me" and "you": "So let me make a deal with you" (Gould 1997:2); "please read this book. Then let's talk" (ibid.:4). A one-to-one tone is also conveyed in Lucretius's *On the Nature of the Universe*, although it stems from a somewhat different literary convention. Specifically, Lucretius addresses his poem to a single dedicatee (Memmius). A reader, of then or now, can readily identify with the poem's named addressee. For a recent folkloristic treatment of self-help literature, see Dolby (2005).

31. For example, Paul Davies (1993) opens his book *The Mind of God* with Hawking's passage, while Horgan (1997:73, 244) picks up on Weinberg's "pointless" comment.

32. Another argument advanced by Lucretius is that atoms also limit the decomposition of matter; without a bedrock of indivisible particles, the matter of the universe would be continually breaking into finer and finer substance, and regeneration would be impossible (see Lucretius 1994:23–24 [1.550–83]).

33. Barrow's book was also re-released in a greatly expanded edition in 2005; the additions do not affect the arguments I present here (Barrow 2005).

34. Thus following the matter, life, and mind progression noted earlier in regard to Freud's triad of heroes.

35. See note 16. Also see Eger (1993:197) on Darwin's place in "the new epic of science."

References

Abrams, Nancy, and Joel Primack. 2011. *The New Universe and the Human Future*. New Haven: Yale University Press.

Achenbach, Joel. 2014. "Star Power." *Smithsonian* 44: 68–78.

Aristotle. 1973. *Poetics*. Ann Arbor: University of Michigan Press.

Barrow, John. 1995. *The Artful Universe*. Oxford: Oxford University Press.

Barrow, John. 2005. *The Artful Universe Expanded*. Oxford: Oxford University Press.

Barthes, Roland. 1995. *Mythologies*. New York: Hill and Wang.

Bascom, William. 1984. "The Forms of Folklore: Prose Narratives." In Alan Dundes, ed., *Sacred Narrative*, 5–29. Berkeley: University of California Press.

Bauman, Richard, and Charles Briggs. 2003. *Voices of Modernity: Language Ideologies and the Politics of Inequality*. Cambridge: Cambridge University Press. http://dx.doi.org /10.1017/CBO9780511486647.

Beckmann, Petr. 1976. *A History of Pi*. New York: St. Martins.

Bierce, Ambrose. 1946. *The Collected Writings of Ambrose Bierce*. New York: Citadel.

Blanchot, Maurice. 1995. *The Writing of the Disaster*. Lincoln: University of Nebraska Press.

Blumenberg, Hans. 1987. *The Genesis of the Copernican World*. Cambridge: MIT Press.

Boas, Franz. 1905. "The Mythologies of the Indians." *International Quarterly* 11: 327–42.

Boslough, John. 1989. *Stephen Hawking's Universe*. New York: Avon.

Brisson, Luc. 2004. *How Philosophers Save Myths*. Chicago: University of Chicago Press. http://dx.doi.org/10.7208/chicago/9780226075389.001.0001.

Brodie, Richard. 2009. *Virus of the Mind*. Carlsbad: Hay House.

Campbell, Joseph. 2004. *The Hero with a Thousand Faces*. Princeton: Princeton University Press.

Capra, Frank. 1997. *The Name above the Title*. Boston: Da Capro.

Chaiken, Andrew. 1998. *A Man on the Moon: The Voyages of the Apollo Astronauts*. New York: Penguin Books.

Comte, Auguste. 1975. *Auguste Comte and Positivism: The Essential Writings*. New York: Harper and Row.

Courlander, Harold. 1987. *The Fourth World of the Hopis*. Albuquerque: University of New Mexico Press.

Davies, Paul. 1993. *The Mind of God: The Scientific Basis for a Rational World*. New York: Touchstone.

Davies, Paul. 2007. *Cosmic Jackpot*. Boston: Houghton Mifflin.

Davis, Mary, et al. 2004. *Mythic Journeys*. Atlanta: Mythic Imagination Institute (program for "Mythic Journeys" conference, June 2–6).

Dawkins, Richard. 1989. *The Selfish Gene*. Oxford: Oxford University Press.

Dawkins, Richard. 1993. "Viruses of the Mind." In Bo Dahlbom, ed., *Dennett and His Critics*, 13–27. Malden: Blackwell.

Dawkins, Richard. 1998. *Unweaving the Rainbow*. Boston: Houghton Mifflin.

Dawkins, Richard. 2003. "Crystalline Truths and Crystal Balls." In *A Devil's Chaplain*, 42–46. Boston: Houghton Mifflin.

DOI: 10.7330/9780874219708.c011

Dawkins, Richard. 2005. *The Ancestor's Tale: Pilgrimage to the Dawn of Evolution.* Boston: Houghton Mifflin.

Dawkins, Richard. 2006. *The God Delusion.* Boston: Houghton Mifflin.

Dennett, Daniel. 1996. *Darwin's Dangerous Idea.* New York: Touchstone.

Dennett, Daniel. 2006. *Breaking the Spell.* New York: Viking.

Distin, Kate. 2005. *The Selfish Meme.* Cambridge: Cambridge University Press.

Dolby, Sandra. 2005. *Self-Help Books: Why Americans Keep Reading Them.* Urbana: University of Illinois Press.

Dolby Stahl, Sandra. 1989. *Literary Folkloristics and the Personal Narrative.* Bloomington: Indiana University Press.

Dundes, Alan. 1968. "The Number Three in American Culture." In Alan Dundes, ed., *Every Man His Way: Readings in Cultural Anthropology*, 401–23. Englewood Cliffs: Prentice-Hall.

Dundes, Alan. 1994. "On the Structure of the Proverb." In Wolfgang Mieder and Alan Dundes, eds., *The Wisdom of Many*, 43–64. Madison: University of Wisconsin Press.

Eger, Martin. 1993. "Hermeneutics and the New Epic of Science." In Murdo William McRae, ed., *The Literature of Science: Perspectives on Popular Scientific Writing*, 186–209. Athens: University of Georgia Press.

El-Shamy, Hasan, and Gregory Schrempp. 2005. "Union of Opposites." In Jane Garry and Hasan El-Shamy, eds., *Archetypes and Motifs in Folklore and Literature: A Handbook*, 481–88. Armonk, NY: North Castle Books.

Feldman, Burton, and Robert Richardson. 1975. *The Rise of Modern Mythology 1680–1860.* Bloomington: Indiana University Press.

Ferris, Timothy, ed. 2001. *The Best American Science Writing.* New York: HarperCollins.

Feynman, Richard. 1985. *"Surely You're Joking, Mr. Feynman!": Adventures of a Curious Character.* New York: W. W. Norton.

Fontenelle, Bernard. 1975 [1724]. *Of the Origin of Fables* [excerpt]. In Burton Feldman and Robert Richardson, eds., *The Rise of Modern Mythology 1680–1860*, 10–18. Bloomington: Indiana University Press.

Frazer, James. 1930. *Myths of the Origin of Fire.* London: Macmillan.

Frazer, James. 1984. "The Fall of Man." In Alan Dundes, ed., *Sacred Narrative*, 72–97. Berkeley: University of California Press.

Freud, Sigmund. 1964. *New Introductory Lectures on Psycho-Analysis and Other Works.* London: Hogarth.

Gale, Monica. 1994. *Myth and Poetry in Lucretius.* Cambridge: Cambridge University Press.

Gelb, Michael J. 1998. *How to Think Like Leonardo da Vinci: Seven Steps to Genius Every Day.* New York: Dell.

Gelb, Michael J. 1999. *The How to Think Like Leonardo da Vinci Workbook: Your Personal Companion to How to Think Like Leonardo da Vinci.* New York: Dell.

Gelb, Michael J. 2002. *Discover Your Genius: How to Think Like History's Ten Most Revolutionary Minds.* New York: HarperCollins.

Gelb, Michael J. 2010. *Wine Drinking for Inspired Thinking: Uncork Your Creative Juices.* Philadelphia: Running Press.

Gilbert, James. 1997. *Redeeming Culture: American Religion in an Age of Science.* Chicago: University of Chicago Press. http://dx.doi.org/10.7208/chicago/9780226293233.001.0001.

Gleick, James. 1987. *Chaos: Making a New Science.* New York: Viking.

Godfrey-Smith, Peter. 2010. *Darwinian Populations and Natural Selection.* Oxford: Oxford University Press.

Godwin, John. 1994. "Introduction." In Lucretius, *On the Nature of the Universe*, ix–xxxii. London: Penguin.

Goldstein, Diane E. 2004. *Once upon a Virus: AIDS Legends and Vernacular Risk Perception.* Logan: Utah State University Press.

Gould, Stephen Jay. 1997. *Full House.* New York: Three Rivers.

Gould, Stephen Jay. 1999. *Rocks of Ages: Science and Religion in the Fullness of Life.* New York: Ballantine.

Gould, Stephen Jay. 2003. "The Narthex of San Marco." In Stephen Jay Gould, *I Have Landed*, 271–84. New York: Three Rivers.

Gould, Stephen Jay, and Richard Charles Lewontin. 1979. "The Spandrels of San Marco and the Panglossian Paradigm: A Critique of the Adaptationist Programme." *Proceedings of the Royal Society of London: Series B, Biological Sciences* 205 (1161): 581–98. http://dx.doi.org/10.1098/rspb.1979.0086.

Greene, Brian. 2000. *The Elegant Universe.* New York: Vintage Books.

Greene, Brian. 2004. *The Fabric of the Cosmos.* New York: Alfred A. Knopf.

Gussow, Mel. 1996. *Conversations with Stoppard.* New York: Grove.

Guthrie, Stewart Eliott. 1993. *Faces in the Clouds.* Oxford: Oxford University Press.

Hawking, Stephen. 1988. *A Brief History of Time.* Toronto: Bantam.

Homer. 1989. *Iliad.* Trans. Robert Fitzgerald. New York: Anchor Books.

Hoover Dam Souvenir Guide. 2003. Lake Mead Magazine.

Horgan, John. 1997. *The End of Science.* New York: Broadway Books.

Hume, David. 2008 [1757]. *The Natural History of Religion.* Oxford: Oxford University Press. http://dx.doi.org/10.1522/030145278.

Kant, Immanuel. 1965. *The Critique of Pure Reason.* New York: St. Martin's.

Keillor, Garrison. 1987. *Leaving Home.* New York: Viking.

Kirk, G. S., J. E. Raven, and M. Schofield. 1983. *The Presocratic Philosophers.* Cambridge: Cambridge University Press.

Kluger, Jeffey. 2012. "The Cathedral of Science." *Time* 180 (4) (July 23): 32–35.

Krauss, Lawrence. 1996. *The Physics of Star Trek.* New York: HarperCollins.

Kuhn, Thomas. 1962. *The Structure of Scientific Revolutions.* Chicago: University of Chicago Press.

Kurtz, Paul. 1997. *The Courage to Become: The Virtues of Humanism.* Westport, CT: Praeger.

Lakoff, George, and Mark Johnson. 1999. *Philosophy in the Flesh.* New York: Basic Books.

Langewiesche, William. 2003. "Columbia's Last Flight: The Inside Story of the Investigation—and the Catastrophe It Laid Bare." *Atlantic Monthly* 292 (4): 58–87.

Latour, Bruno. 1993. *We Have Never Been Modern.* Cambridge: Harvard University Press.

Lévi-Strauss, Claude. 1967a. "The Structural Study of Myth." In Claude Lévi-Strauss, *Structural Anthropology*, 202–28. Garden City: Anchor Books.

Lévi-Strauss, Claude. 1967b. "Do Dual Organizations Exist?" In Claude Lévi-Strauss, *Structural Anthropology*, 128–60. Garden City: Anchor Books.

Lévi-Strauss, Claude. 1967c. "Split Representation in the Art of Asia and America." In Claude Lévi-Strauss, *Structural Anthrpology*, 239–63. Garden City: Anchor Books.

Lévi-Strauss, Claude. 1970a. *The Savage Mind.* Chicago: University of Chicago Press.

Lévi-Strauss, Claude. 1970b. *The Raw and the Cooked.* New York: Harper and Row.

Lévi-Strauss, Claude. 1971. "The Story of Asdiwal." In Edmund Leach, ed., *The Structural Study of Myth and Totemism*, 1–48. London: Tavistock.

Levy, Joel. 2011. *A Bee in a Cathedral and 99 Other Scientific Analogies.* Buffalo: Firefly Books.

Lincoln, Bruce. 2000. *Theorizing Myth.* Chicago: University of Chicago Press.

Lucretius. 1994. *On the Nature of the Universe.* London: Penguin. Translation of *De Rerum Natura.* Trans. R. E. Latham; rev. John Godwin.

Maclean, Norman. 1976. "A River Runs through It." In Norman Maclean, *A River Runs through It and Other Stories*, 1–104. Chicago: University of Chicago Press.

Malinowski, Bronislaw. 1961. *Argonauts of the Western Pacific*. New York: E. P. Dutton.

Manuel, Frank. 1959. *The Eighteenth Century Confronts the Gods*. Cambridge: Harvard University Press.

Margolis, Howard. 2002. *It Started with Copernicus: How Turning the World Inside Out Led to the Scientific Revolution*. New York: McGraw-Hill.

McBride, Joseph. 2000. *Frank Capra: The Catastrophe of Success*. New York: St. Martin's.

McKay, Lori. 2004. "Letter to the Editor." *Atlantic Monthly* 293 (1) (January-February): 16–18.

Mieder, Wolfgang. 2004a. "Proverb Pictures Are Worth More than a Thousand Words: From Pieter Bruegel's 'Netherlandish Proverbs' to T. E. Breitenbach's 'Proverbidioms.' Paper presented at the American Folklore Society annual meeting, October 13–17, Salt Lake City, Utah.

Mieder, Wolfgang. 2004b. " 'One Picture That's Worth More than a Thousand Words': Pieter Bruegel the Elder's *Netherlandish Proverbs*—Past and Present." In Wolfgang Mieder, ed., *The Netherlandish Proverbs: An International Symposium on the Pieter Brueg(h)els*, 195–241. Burlington: University of Vermont.

Nelkin, Dorothy. 1995. *Selling Science*. New York: W. H. Freeman.

Numazawa, K. 1984. "The Cultural-Historical Background of Myths and the Separation of Sky and Earth." In Alan Dundes, ed., *Sacred Narrative*, 182–92. Berkeley: University of California Press.

Olrik, Axel. 1965. "Epic Laws of Folk Narrative." In Alan Dundes, ed., *The Study of Folklore*, 129–41. Englewood Cliffs: Prentice-Hall.

Packard, Edward. 1994. *Imagining the Universe: A Visual Journey*. New York: Perigee.

Parsons, Talcott, and Edward Shils. 1951. *Toward a General Theory of Action*. Cambridge: Harvard University Press. http://dx.doi.org/10.4159/harvard.9780674863507.

Pinker, Steven. 1995. *The Language Instinct*. New York: HarperCollins.

Pinker, Steven. 2011. *The Better Angels of Our Nature: Why Violence Has Declined*. New York: Viking.

Plato. 1985. *The Republic*. Trans. Richard W. Sterling and William C. Scott. New York: W. W. Norton.

Porter, Eliot, and James Gleick. 1990. *Nature's Chaos*. New York: Viking.

Primack, Joel, and Nancy Ellen Abrams. 2006. *The View from the Center of the Universe*. New York: Riverhead Books.

Propp, Vladimir. 1958. *The Morphology of the Folktale*. Austin: University of Texas Press.

Ranke, Kurt. 1967. "Einfache Formen." *Journal of the Folklore Institute* 4 (1): 17–31. http://dx.doi.org/10.2307/3813910.

Ray, Darrel. 2009. *The God Virus: How Religion Infects Our Lives and Culture*. Bonner Springs, KS: IPC Press.

Sagan, Carl. 1994. *Pale Blue Dot*. New York: Random House.

Sagan, Carl. 1996. *The Demon-Haunted World: Science as a Candle in the Dark*. New York: Ballantine Books.

Scherle, Victor, and William Levy. 1977. *The Films of Frank Capra*. Secaucus: Citadel.

Schrempp, Gregory. 1983. "The Re-education of Friedrich Max Müller: Intellectual Appropriation and Epistemological Antinomy in Mid-Victorian Evolutinary Thought." *Man* 18 (1): 90–110. http://dx.doi.org/10.2307/2801766.

Schrempp, Gregory. 1992. *Magical Arrows: The Maori, the Greeks, and the Folklore of the Universe*. Madison: University of Wisconsin Press.

Schrempp, Gregory. 2012a. *The Ancient Mythology of Modern Science: A Mythologist Looks (Seriously) at Popular Science Writing*. Montreal: McGill-Queens University Press.

Schrempp, Gregory. 2012b. "Mythology and Science; or, What Do We Want from Popular Science?" *Huffington Post* [Science] (October 8). At http://www.huffingtonpost.com/gregory-schrempp/myths-and-science_b_1949316.html.

Secrets of the Universe. 1999. Pittsburgh: International Masters.

Shneiderman, Ben. 2003. *Leonardo's Laptop: Human Needs and the New Computing Technologies.* Cambridge: MIT Press.

Stocking, George. 1968. *Race, Culture, and Evolution.* New York: Free Press.

Stoppard, Tom. 1974. *Jumpers.* New York: Grove.

Stoppard, Tom. 1976. *The Real Inspector Hound.* London: Faber and Faber.

Thompson, Stith. 1955–58. *Motif-Index of Folk-Literature.* Bloomington: Indiana University Press.

Tylor, E. B. 1871. *Primitive Culture,* 2 vols. London: John Murray.

Updike, John. 2000. *More Matter.* New York: Alfred A. Knopf.

Vernant, Jean-Pierre. 1984. *The Origins of Greek Thought.* Ithaca: Cornell University Press.

Volk, Katharina. 2002. *The Poetics of Latin Didactic.* Oxford: Oxford University Press. http://dx.doi.org/10.1093/acprof:oso/9780199245505.001.0001.

Weber, Max. 1958. *The Protestant Ethic and the Spirit of Captialism.* New York: Charles Scribner's Sons.

Weinberg, Steven. 1984. *The First Three Minutes.* Toronto: Bantam.

Weinberg, Steven. 2003. *Facing Up: Science and Its Cultural Adversaries.* Cambridge: Harvard University Press.

Weinstein, Lawrence, and John A. Adam. 2008. *Guesstimation.* Princeton: Princeton University Press.

White, Michael, and John Bribben. 1992. *Stephen Hawking: A Life in Science.* London: Viking.

Wilson, Edward O. 1998. *Conscilience.* New York: Alfred A. Knopf.

Young, Louise. 1993. *The Unfinished Universe.* Oxford: Oxford University Press.

Zipes, Jack. 2006. *Why Fairy Tales Stick.* New York: Routledge.

Zipes, Jack. 2008. "What Makes a Repulsive Frog So Appealing: Memetics and Fairy Tales." *Journal of Folklore Research* 45 (2): 109–43. http://dx.doi.org/10.2979/JFR.2008.45.2.109.

Filmography

Cosmos. 2000. Carl Sagan, narrator. Cosmos Studios, Inc. DVD.

Faith and Reason. 1998. Margaret Wertheim, writer and host. New River Media in association with Five Continents Music, Inc. VHS.

Hemo the Magnificent. 1957. Dir. Frank Capra. MMIII Image Entertainment, Inc. DVD.

Our Mr. Sun. 1956. Dir. Frank Capra. MMIII Image Entertainment, Inc. DVD.

The Strange Case of the Cosmic Rays. 1957. Dir. Frank Capra. MMIII Image Entertainment, Inc. DVD.

The Unchained Goddess. 1958. Dir. Frank Capra. MMIII Image Entertainment, Inc. DVD.

About the Author

Gregory Schrempp is professor in the Department of Folklore and Ethnomusicology at Indiana University (Bloomington), where he teaches courses in mythology, comparative cosmology, and intellectual history. He has carried out archival and field research in Polynesian cosmologies, emphasizing Maori. He is author of *The Ancient Mythology of Modern Science: A Mythologist Looks (Seriously) at Popular Science Writing* (2012) and *Magical Arrows: The Maori, the Greeks, and the Folklore of the Universe* (1992).

Index